# FALLS FROM GRACE

Also by Michael Adzema

From the Return to Grace series

*Culture War, Class War.* Volume 1
*Apocalypse Emergency.* Volume 3
*Apocalypse NO.* Volume 4
*Planetmates: The Great Reveal.* Volume 6
*Experience Is Divinity.* Volume 8

*Wounded Deer and Centaurs.* Volume 5 (forthcoming)
*Funny God.* Volume 7 (forthcoming)
*Prodigal Human.* Volume 10 (forthcoming)

# FALLS FROM GRACE

## THE DEVOLUTION AND REVOLUTION OF CONSCIOUSNESS

Return to Grace, Volume 9

## MICHAEL ADZEMA

*To indigenous and "primal" peoples of all kinds everywhere.*

# CONTENTS

CONTENTS

# ACKNOWLEDGMENTS

I wish to acknowledge, first and foremost, my wife, Mary Lynn Adzema. It was her support and companionship, while the bulk of the original writings that formed this book were conceived, which made it possible. Together we participated in Grof Transpersonal Training workshops. She was my sitter for all of the sessions of holotropic breathwork that I describe in this book. She was my partner in our primal breathwork workshops, too. Her quiet wisdom and solid support infused all of those activities. She has been a sounding board for all the ideas of this book, as it took shape over the last twenty-five years.

The book's origins, however, go back to my days as an undergraduate at Franklin and Marshall College in 1969 through '72. Richard French was the professor, the pied piper, who inspired me off my predetermined course of mathematics onto a much more radical one of self-understanding — psychology, philosophy, and spiritual studies.

I wish to thank Arthur Janov for bringing the revolutionary modality for personal growth of primal therapy to the world. It has immeasurably transformed my life and given me one that there is no way I would have been able to experience or achieve without the benefit of such a thorough process of unencumbering of emotional leftovers and re-membering of once separated aspects of Self.

I need to thank Jules and Helen Roth of the Denver Primal Center, for making the facility available, and for the training and wisdom they imparted to all the facilitators I worked with there. A special nod goes to Warren A. Baker, M.D., as he was my therapist for my three-week Intensive, which started the primal process. Affection to Kathy Buchenauer and Emily Easton for their support and contributions to my process there. And to Hollis Orr for her important supportive role in my continued process after Denver.

Sharon Coggan was especially helpful while the ideas that became Section Two of this book were fomenting. As my primary advisor for my program at the University of Colorado at Denver in humanistic psychology, she was an active participant in the hashing out of my cumulative project, "A Primal Perspective on Spirituality"; and without her insistence and prod, in 1979 at its completion, I might never have submitted it to the *Journal of Humanistic Psychology,* where it was eventually published in 1985, in all its length and breadth.

Who to thank for my initial experiences of cellular consciousness, in particular, sperm memory? No one, except the Universe or Divine Intent. For I had only read a few sentences in a couple places about the possibility of such events before they happened to me. And for years, I had no support or confirmation from the outside on the things I was experiencing. Indeed, when I first heard about Graham Farrant's research, I felt such a relief and such a weight of responsibility for these ideas, not exactly lifted, but at least shared. Later, as this book attests, there would be more and more validation of these ideas.

Still, I need to acknowledge Robin McGinn's assistance as sitter in my absolute first such sperm memory. And with great affection I want to mention Bruce Stockton. He was my friend and housemate at the time and happened to be in his room, adjoining mine, at the time of my first such experience. The experience happened during a primal buddying session — a "re-experiencing" session — with Robin McGinn in my primal box, inside of my room, and he did not know I was having a session. He was entertaining his young son, approximately five years old, who was on a visit. After Robin left and I joined Bruce in his room and conveyed the story of my sperm experience and expressed my astonishment, he smiled knowingly. He said only two words, "I know." Then he picked up a piece of paper on which his son had drawn a picture of me — complete with glasses — as a sperm. Such confirming synchronicity abounds at the cellular-transpersonal level of the psyche.

Stanislav Grof and Christina Grof have had a huge influence on all that is in this book. Through my participation in the Grof Training for holotropic breathwork, I was facilitated in the experiences which comprise Section Three of this book, "A Foray Into Cellular-Transpersonal Consciousness." Stanislav Grof's writings have played importantly into the development of the theories and perspectives advanced in this text. Without his ground-breaking work into the deep unconscious, I do not see how I would have had the elements with which to conceive the foundation of the ideas in this book. Without the modality of holotropic breathwork, which he has made available, I do not know how I would have opened to the realities and insights that stimulated these additional perspectives of the deep unconscious, the Self, the process of spirituality, and the further reaches and earliest origins of consciousness at the cellular level of experience.

Jarvin Heiman, M.D., who offered regular workshops in holotropic breathwork, set the stage for and oversaw my first and transformative experiences in that modality. One experience of very real "heart opening" happened in one workshop and alone transformed my life. I remember with great affection and appreciation Amber Williams and so many Grof Transpersonal Training trainees, with whom I learned and facilitated.

I wish to acknowledge the support and encouragement of my thesis advisor, Philip Clayton, as I cobbled together the parts of my writings that became, first, my Master's thesis, and later, the book, *Falls from Grace*.

Eventually I met up with and did training in primal therapy with Graham Farrant. His ideas, expressed through his colleague, Terry Larimore, and his appearance at a PPPANA conference had already fortified my renderings, and I had shared manuscripts with him and published his work in the psychology journals (*Aesthema* and *Primal Renaissance*) of which I was the editor. When I last bid him adieu, and, shaking my hand, he instructed me to "bring primal therapy into the twenty-first century," I do not believe he was at all aware that he had a deadly disease, which would take his life only a few years hence. The late Terry Larimore, my dear, dear friend, also played an important role in educating people on cellular-transpersonal consciousness.

I have deep gratitude to Elizabeth Noble and Paul Hannig who in their works have supported this idea of cellular consciousness and conveyed frameworks within which they are understandable ... doing their part, as it were, to "bring primal into the twenty-first century." Their ideas have assisted the development of my own. Last but not least, Sathya Sai Baba's many works and personal influence on my life have assisted this work, especially in providing a rare vision of a Reality outside these falls from grace, one untainted by Pain ... of Bliss, Beauty, and Awareness unimaginable.

In the actual production of this book, I want to mention Mary Lynn Adzema's help in editing and as sounding board on ideas. I want to give a special shout out to Attila Vajda, who provided input on the cover.

I wish to express my appreciation to my friend, Ceila Starshine Levine, for being part of many discussions around this book and its ideas for several decades now, and for being a sounding board for some of it. Peter Radford, my stepson and friend, has also, with acumen and wisdom, engaged in many deep interactions around these ideas, and so benefited this work. I want to acknowledge the staunch support, intellectual and personal, I receive on all my publications and ideas from dear friends, Debbie Condon and Mary Elizabeth Dupont. Such feedback, appreciation, and alliance, in a field sparse with aficionados, let alone adepts ... or congratulators ... could not be more welcome and appreciated.

Finally, thanks are due all the people I will never meet in person on the internet and especially Facebook who have reviewed and commented on every aspect of this book — contents to cover. The feedback and input I received from, literally, thousands of minds over the last two years as I posted all parts of this book has no doubt raised this work above what I would have achieved on my own.

# INTRODUCTION

## The Radical Rational View of Us and It: "Normal" Truth Is Convenient Truth … and Is Anything But True

*Prenatal Spirituality and the Devolutional Model of Consciousness: A Revolution in Child Development, Parenting, Mental Health, and Spirituality Is at Hand*

## "Normal" Truth Is Convenient Truth … and Is Anything But True

*Falls from Grace* presents a radical theory of spirituality, evolution, child development, stages of life, purpose of life, human nature, and the human species. It is a comprehensive theory, which basically turns everything on its head to find the truth. For its premise is that human ego is a filter to truth and so, for the most part, turns truth into falsehood and vice-versa. Thus truth outside of ego, absolute truth — what exists when ego needs are filtered out — often ends up being the opposite of what humans' egos have propounded as self-evident. Seemingly unimpeachable, these "normal" truths are only convenient truth, in actuality. They are meant to placate and prop up the human ego and have nothing to do with truth outside of that psychological need.

Still, while *Falls from Grace* is a radical view, it is in line with mystical beliefs, platonic thought, and even much of primitive or primal-like views of the world and Nature. Beyond that, however, it finds the roots of ideas of soul, myth, and spirituality at our earliest beginnings and in a cellular consciousness. In doing so this work is a reconciliation of divergent views in the fields of prenatal and perinatal and transpersonal psychology.

# Falls from Grace — Description and Overview

This work brings the new information of prenatal and perinatal psychology to bear upon basic spiritual and philosophical constructs regarding the nature of consciousness, child development, personal growth, and transpersonal "evolution."

## A Devolutional Model of Consciousness and Development

It utilizes the results of the phenomenon of re-experience of events surrounding and preceding one's birth, as well as the more empirically rooted findings concerning our origins and our earliest experiences, into a coherent structure for understanding their implications. This structure is a *devolutional* model, meaning that the normal process of development is seen as a regression from or "forgetting" of prior, more aware states.

## Prenatal Spirituality

After an initial overview of the field of *prenatal and perinatal psychology*, in Section One, that review of the current understanding and findings in this area is built upon in making a case for the legitimacy of *prenatal spirituality*. Prenatal spirituality means basically two things: (1) that regression to prenatal and perinatal states represents a spiritual progression and a proximity to and increased access of spiritual states and awareness; and (2) that these earliest events themselves, as they originally occurred, were characterized by a similar heightened spiritual proximity and awareness.

Making this case is important for two reasons: For one, there is a strong tradition in the field of re-experience that reduces all spirituality and spiritual experiences to early traumas and neurosis. This is the dominant attitude in psychoanalysis, articulated initially by Freud. However it has been carried and promulgated forcefully into the field of re-experience by Arthur Janov — one of the field's leading theorists. This idea that all spirituality is derivative of underlying primal pain, as Janov contends, is addressed and disputed here.

Second, just as spirituality and spiritual experience are denigrated in the light of primal experience by Arthur Janov, on the flip side of this Ken Wilber denigrates primal and prenatal experience in the light of spiritual experience. Wilber — the dominant theoretician in the field of *transpersonal psychology* — claims that preverbal states, like primal and prenatal re-experience, are the opposite of transverbal states — what he considers to be true spiritual experience. I focus on and dispute this aspect of Wilber's thinking in making the case for prenatal spirituality in Section Two, but also throughout this work. That prenatal states are identical to, akin to, or at least leading to transpersonal states and that Ken Wilber has made a major mistake in contending the contrary is a central theme of this book.

Thus, the idea, presented initially — that there exists prenatal and cellular consciousness as well as an inherent spirituality or proximity to the numinous and transpersonal, if not also divinity, at these levels of development — is a crucial idea in all that follows. This case is made, in Section Two, on the basis of the available evidence in relevant fields and in particular from the viewpoint of findings in primal therapy.

## Where Primal Re-Experience and Transpersonal Experience Meet

What will follow this analysis of the case for prenatal spirituality are examples of it from my own re-experience through the modality of *holotropic breathwork*$^{TM}$ — a technique of transpersonal access and reliving developed by Stanislav and Christina Grof. These pages, in Section Three, should be seen as providing a sample of the sorts of experiences, insights, and perspectives that can occur through the phenomenon of re-experience. Though no sample could possibly represent the essence, expanse, or necessary outline of this highly individual and vastly diverse level of experience, my own experiences demonstrate clearly the overlap between the personal and transpersonal — between the biographical/biological and the spiritual/numinous — that characterizes this arena of experience.

## "Normal" "Development" Is Devolutional for It Is About Gradual Separation from Divinity

Following immediately afterwards, Sections Four through Eight, are the sections that present the ontogenetic model of consciousness and *devolutional* — meaning the opposite of evolution — development based on such inquiry. It is the heart of the vision of this book. This part, Part 2, titled "Falls From Grace," details a process of removal from divinity or a higher state during the process of coming into this world as a series of stages — four stages, in fact. These stages center on the events of conception, birth, the primal scene (around age four or five), and puberty or the identity stage. Astonishingly, they happen to correspond to Wilber's (1977) levels of consciousness in his "spectrum of consciousness."

Implications of This Are for an Overthrow of the Usual Ideas of Child Development, Parenting, Personal Growth, Psychotherapy, and Spiritual Evolution

Finally, what follows — Part 3 — is a presentation of the implications of this model for child development and parenting, for psychotherapy and personal growth, and for spiritual evolution and higher consciousness. This part carries forward some of the themes presented thus far to their logical conclusions in terms of their effects on current models and thinking and on society and culture. The earliest indications are that the implications from including the prenatal and primal perspective are vast. For indeed this new perspective, this new information seems to call for an overthrow, or at least a reversal, of many of the aspects of the dominant paradigms in parenting, child development, psychotherapy, and spiritual growth.

# A Radical New Vision — Prenatal and Perinatal Psychology

So, now we look at an overview of the field of pre- and perinatal psychology. The findings from this new field of science make possible this radical new vision into ourselves, our place in the Universe, the purposes of our lives, and the directions along which our efforts to better ourselves might most fruitfully be aligned.

# PART 1

# PRENATAL PSYCHOLOGY AND SPIRITUALITY

SECTION ONE


# PRENATAL AND PERINATAL PSYCHOLOGY AND THE PHENOMENON OF RE-EXPERIENCE

# Your Map of Reality Was Written in the Womb: Foundations of Myth and Mind and My Personal Involvement with This Research into Our Actual "Human Nature"

*Everything You "Know" About Life You Learned as a Fetus: Prenatal and Perinatal Psychology and the Phenomenon of Re-Experience*

## Prenatal and Perinatal Psychology and the Phenomenon of Re-Experience

*Prenatal and perinatal psychology* is the field that deals with the effects of events occurring prior to (*prenatal*) and surrounding (*perinatal*) the time of birth upon later life and personality. An ever increasing amount though certainly not all of the information we have about these periods of our lives and their effects is derived through the later and vivid remembering of these events in a phenomenon known as *re-experience*. Correspondingly, the two most frequently asked questions about this relatively new field, put by those initially encountering it, are those concerning the specific meanings of the terms *perinatal* and *re-experience*.

At the outset, I wish to present an explanation of these two terms and of my unique personal relation to this topic as well as some of my background in exploring it. I will follow this with an historical overview of the field of prenatal and perinatal psychology, which will reveal the key concepts and understandings employed throughout this book.

## Re-Experience and Reliving

For over forty years, beginning in 1972 when I was a senior undergraduate in college, I have been involved both personally and professionally in a comprehensive investigation into the phenomenon of *re-experience*. Also called *reliving*, this phenomenon is reported to consist of a *full somato-cognitive remembering of previous events in a person's life*. Reliving involves experiential but also observable and measurable components, such as brain wave changes, characteristic physiological and neurological changes, and typical observable body movements.

This phenomenon can occur, to varying degrees, in many consciousness-altering modalities — including hypnosis, LSD psychotherapy, primal therapy, rebirthing, and holotropic breathwork; to a considerable degree in re-evaluation co-counseling and treatment for post-traumatic stress disorder; and, occasionally and spontaneously, even in mainstream forms of psychotherapy, counseling, and "growth seminars."

Re-experience is a more vivid and more completely somatic catharsis than what has been described in psychotherapy in terms of *abreaction*. It is in such contrast to normal abreaction that when these seemingly bizarre yet healing events have spontaneously erupted in traditional or mainstream Western contexts they have usually been mistakenly labeled *psychotic*, been intervened upon, and then aborted — via drugs and other highly coercive measures — by the attending therapeutic authorities.

However, with an increasing appreciation for their therapeutic value, these events are gradually becoming understood and accepted in therapeutic contexts and thus allowed to complete themselves and to instruct the participants and observers in their meanings. Therefore, they appear to represent something new in our culture in terms of both a way of approaching knowledge and in terms of the kinds of information that are discovered (Grof 1976, 1985; Hannig 1982; Janov 1971; Lake 1966/1986; Noble, 1993; Stettbacher, 1992).

# My Relationship to the Phenomenon of Re-Experience

My interest in the phenomenon of reliving began forty-four years ago at Franklin and Marshall College in Lancaster, Pennsylvania. As an undergraduate there I was most inspired by a course offered in the religious studies department titled "Religious and Psychological Approaches To Self-Understanding." I was so inspired by the course that I constructed my major around its topic and initially even used the same title for my program's name. This major in "self-understanding" would lead me, in a few years, to a profound interest in and exploration of primal therapy, as presented by Arthur Janov (1970) in his much-publicized book, *The Primal Scream: Primal Therapy: The Cure for Neurosis*.

By 1972, I had completed all but the one final semester for a B.A. That semester was to include the cumulative project — required of such a Special Studies (individually structured) major. However, since my project would focus on primal therapy and one of primal therapy's basic premises is that knowledge cannot really be known except through experience, I could not in good conscience turn in a project describing primal therapy without first experiencing it. Consequently I withdrew from college, for what was supposed to

7

be only a semester, with the intention of "going through" primal therapy and then returning to school to write my cumulative project on it. In those days, the entire process of primal therapy was reputed to take only three to six months.

But a lot was unknown about that modality in those early days. As it turned out, I would not return to school to complete that final project until 1978 — at which point I had five years' experience of primal therapy behind me and was living in Denver, Colorado.

In addition to these experiences, I have amassed a broad array of other experience and training over the years that have contributed to my understanding of re-experience and of this field in general. Besides my two decades and more of primal therapy ... both formally and in "the buddy system" ... I have received training as a primal therapist. I am also a trained rebirther, having explored that modality since 1986. I have been experientially exploring the modality of holotropic breathwork since 1987 and did training with Stanislav and Christina Grof in that technique.

Finally, I have been facilitating people in their journeys into deep inner primal and holotropic states since 1975. I have given individual sessions in all three modalities of primal therapy, rebirthing, and holotropic breathwork. And with my wife, Mary Lynn Adzema, I conducted three day workshops in something we called primal breathwork. I have also conducted two-day group workshops in this modality at conferences, which were attended by as many as sixty experiencers at a time.

Thus, I have experience in my own process in these modalities; but in addition I have facilitated for others on many occasions, and at times, it was my main profession — though most of my life I have spent in writing, teaching, and research.

# Prenatal and Perinatal Re-Experience

Re-experience of birth and of the events immediately prior to and after birth are termed *perinatal* — from the Greek, literally

8

"surrounding birth." It has been widely described at this point by a number of authors but is most closely associated with the work of Stanislav Grof, Arthur Janov, and Frank Lake.

However, one significant and as yet little explored or understood phenomenon, arising also from the modalities mentioned, is that of *prenatal* re-experience. In this case, the experiencer reports ... and observationally appears to be ... experiencing events that happened *en utero*, sometimes going back as far as sperm, egg, and zygote states (Buchheimer 1987; Farrant 1987; Grof 1976, 1985; Hannig 1982; Janov 1983; Lake 1981, 1982; Larimore 1990a, 1990b; Larimore & Farrant, 1995).

These reports of remembering experiences that occurred before birth are at such variance with Western professional and popular paradigms that they are met with near-universal incredulity and, too often, premature dismissal. Yet the evidence from the mounting numbers of experiential reports and empirical studies attests that something which is at least unique and interesting is going on here.

Nevertheless, much of this prenatal information is thus far unformulated, untheorized, and unintegrated into a coherent structure for making sense of these experiences. This book will go a long way toward doing just that — making sense of prenatal experiences and exploring the implications and prospects of the knowledge gleaned from this fascinating new area of research and which arises from the vision that an exposure to this material induces.

The present work represents an attempt to bring this new information concerning our origins and our earliest experiences into such a coherent structure. After the initial overview of the field to be presented in this section, I deepen that review of the current understanding and findings in this area in making a case, in Section Two, for the legitimacy of prenatal *spirituality.*

First, let us take a closer look at what we know about the time before and around birth and what it means for us throughout our lives.

# 2

# Overview of the Prenatal and Perinatal Psychology Field — Early Theorists: Psychoanalysis and Birth

*Birth trauma creates a feeling of a paradise lost, a separation anxiety, and a futile and lifelong struggle to re-unite with that golden age and that early beloved and to return to the womb.-*

## Sigmund Freud

### Birth as Prototype for All Anxiety

While Sigmund Freud (1927) disregarded major effects of birth on personality, he still saw the birth experience as the prototype of all later anxiety. His overall disregard of birth, however, was largely influenced by the belief — although discredited (see Chamberlain, 1988), still common in mainstream psychology and medicine today — that a newborn does not possess the neurological capacity for consciousness at birth.

# Otto Rank

## Psychoanalysis, Birth Trauma, Foundations of Personality and Some Myth, Separation Anxiety

Other early psychoanalysts disagreed with Freud on this. Otto Rank is the most notable of these. Following Freud's basic psychoanalytic reasoning for personality patterns in early infancy, he asserted basic patterns of experience and ideas that are rooted in even earlier experience. Rank (1929) claimed the deepest, most fundamental patterns of these personality constructs originated at the time of birth, which Freud thought was not possible. Based upon the dream, fantasy, and other patterns of associations arising in his patients in psychoanalysis, Rank postulated a birth trauma, which he saw as a critical event in laying down in each of us particular patterns of thinking, motivation, and emotion for the rest of our lives. Notable among these prototypes was a feeling of a paradise once known but somehow lost, a separation anxiety caused by the separation at birth, and a resulting futile and lifelong struggle to re-unite with that golden age and that early beloved because of a desire to return to the womb.

# Nandor Fodor

## Dreamwork, Birth and Prenatal Processing and Relivings, Prenatal Origins of Consciousness and Trauma

Also a psychoanalyst, Nandor Fodor (1949) focused on the reflections of birth and prenatal material in dreams. He also designed interventions in therapy to release the negative effects of birth and to process prenatal memories. He was the first to mention actual relivings of birth, in which veridical memories were recovered. He agreed with Rank on many points, but he stressed the origins of consciousness and of trauma being in the prenatal period.

# Donald W. Winnicott

First Primal Therapist? Birth Relivings, Importance of Birth — Negative Imprints but Positive Effects, Too

Another psychoanalyst, and pediatrician as well, Winnicott (1958) also held that birth is remembered and is important. He insisted that the birth trauma is real, but he disagreed with Rank and Fodor that it is always traumatic. He suggested that a normal, nontraumatic, birth has many positive benefits, particularly for ego development. Still, he contended that traumatic birth is permanently etched in memory and leaves a lifetime psychological scar. Winnicott (1958) also suggested the possibility of prenatal trauma.

He has been called the first primal therapist in that he described the first *birth primals* — actual observable relivings of birth — spontaneously occurring by some of his patients during their sessions with him. Thus he was beginning the trend beyond mere talking association or dream analysis as ways of accessing and integrating this material.

# 3

# Overview of the Prenatal and Perinatal Psychology Field — Later Research and Theorists: Hypnosis, Primal Therapy, and Birth

*The cutting of the umbilical cord was said to be the true origin of castration fears…. "Birth is like death to the newborn."*

## David Cheek and Leslie LeCron

### Hypnosis, Birth Memories and Imprints on Personality and Relation to Psychiatric Disorders

Cheek and LeCron (1968) used hypnosis to retrieve early memories in their patients. They discovered that memories earlier than what they expected, going back to birth, were possible. Importantly, a relief of symptoms seemed to follow from the re-experience of these birth memories. They came to the conclusion that a birth imprint occurs, which is induced by the extreme stress of that time and is resistant to fading from later experience. Further they asserted that this imprint could be the cause of a wide spectrum of psychiatric and psychosomatic disorders.

# Leslie Feher

## Psychoanalysis, Birth, Cutting of Umbilical Cord, Separation Trauma

Leslie Feher (1980) sought to extend the Freudian tradition farther back into areas that, she asserts, were until only recently unknowable. Thus, she describes a natal theory and therapy that includes experiences of cutting the umbilical cord, birth, and even prebirth. In fact, she considers the cutting of the umbilical cord to be central in her theory of trauma, calling it the "crisis umbilicus," and echoes Fodor in claiming that it is the true origin of the castration fears made so much of in psychoanalysis. This is so because, according to Feher, the cord and placenta is an object of security and is considered by the fetus to be part of him- or herself. Thus, this cutting represents a supreme threat in being a separation from a total life support system, a major organ, a part of oneself. In these ways, she also brings forward for renewed appreciation Rank's speculations on the element of separation trauma as a crucial element of the birth trauma.

# Arthur Janov

## Primal Therapy, Traumas of Birth and Early Life and Healing Them, Empirical Foundations and Neurophysiology of Early Events and Healing

Perhaps the major theorist and popularizer of the phenomenon of re-experience (which he termed *primaling*), Janov was reluctant to acknowledge the pervasiveness of pre- and perinatal re-experience and trauma. Yet when he did, it was in a major work on birth trauma, which remains as a touchstone in the field in its depth and detail. *Imprints: The Lifelong Effects of the Birth Experience*, published in 1983, among other things places birth as the determining factor in creating basic personality constructs, called *sympathetic* and *parasympathetic*, which roughly coincide with the more common terms *introversion* and *extroversion*.

This work is more empirical and neurophysiologically rooted than most in the field. While the book is recognized in the field, Janov and his work have not gotten anywhere near the respect and attention that they deserve. He remains the unfortunate kicking-boy of a movement that is itself scapegoated by the academy and the larger scientific community.

# Thomas Verny

## Primal Therapy, Birth, Especially Womb Life and Relation to Personality … Prenatal Mother-Infant Bonding

The actual stimulus for a new field of pre- and perinatal psychology and the Association for Pre- and Perinatal Psychology and Health (APPPAH) was Thomas Verny's (1981) *The Secret Life of the Unborn Child*. His work brought together a good deal of the new empirical research that had opened the doors to us on the events in the womb. While himself a practitioner of "holistic primal therapy," he integrated the accumulating data from the phenomenon of re-experience with the new information from the more traditional, "objective," scientific research into the prenatal — made possible by the latest advances in technology.

One of his conclusions from this combination of lines of inquiry was that "birth and prenatal experiences form the foundations of human personality" (1981, p. 118). His other conclusions center around the importance of intrauterine bonding in that his research strongly suggests that the prenate, via pathways hormonal and unknown, picks up on the thoughts, feelings, and attitudes of the mother. More importantly, he asserted, the imprint of these factors on the fetus predetermines the later mother-child relationship. He emphasized that positive thoughts and feelings toward the fetus — "maternal love" — acts to cushion the new individual against the normal stresses and unavoidable harshness inherent in birth and early infancy. Yet all of this cannot be completely avoided. "Birth is like death to the newborn," writes Verny (1984, p. 48).

# David Chamberlain

## Hypnosis, Confirmed Validity of Birth Memories

David Chamberlain (1988), for many years the president of APPPAH (the Association for Prenatal and Perinatal Psychology and Health), has further substantiated the claim of consciousness at birth and the accuracy of pre- and perinatal memory in the phenomenon of re-experience. He reported one study he did in which he compared hypnotically retrieved memories of birth from mother and child and found an astonishing degree of conformity in their responses. Of note was the degree of inner consistency and originality in these memories as reported by the former neonate. They often contained technical details of the delivery and labor unlike what would be expected of the medically unsophisticated, a perceptive critique of the way the birth was handled, and other details of the event that could not have been known through normal conscious channels.

# 4

# Overview of the Prenatal and Perinatal Psychology Field — Later Theorists: Societal Implications, Psychohistory, Birth, and Prenatal

*A reduction in awareness as a result of early traumatic events beginning around conception ... cellular patterns that underlie and unite all of reality at all levels of manifestation....*

## Lloyd deMause

### Psychohistory, Prenatal Imprints and Poisonous Placenta, Sociohistorical Implications of Gestational and Birth Events

Lloyd deMause (1982, 1987) was instrumental in establishing the new interdisciplinary field of psychohistory. In his study of historical happenings he discovered that stages in the progression of events related to stages in the progression of gestation and birth

... which stages happened to correspond, by the way, remarkably well with Stanislav Grof's four stages of birth — his Basic Perinatal Matrices.

He found that natal imagery especially predominates in societies during times of crisis and war, when national purpose and state of affairs are construed as a need to escape or break free from an enclosing and constricting force. He also noted the *suffering fetus* and the *poisonous placenta* as sources of these later metaphors and imagery. In fact, in studying the imagery in the national media of various countries he has been able to predict political, social, and economic events such as wars and invasions, recessions, and political downfalls.

His work begins to look at the prenatal influences and imprints and how they related to macrocosmic issues of politics, history, social movements, and issues of war and peace.

# Later Theorists — Dream Analysis

## Francis Mott

### Conception and Gestational Basis of Myth, Archetype, all Patterns of Macrocosmic and Microcosmic Realities and the Nature of Reality, Devolutional Model of Development

Francis Mott's work is less well known even by this field's standards, yet it is undeniably impressive. Mott's (1960, 1964) major contribution lies in his focusing on basic patterns of mind and cosmos that correlate with prenatal feelings and states. He traced consciousness back to events around conception and saw these events as instituting patterns affecting all later experience and conceptual constructions. Through dream analysis he elicited these "configurations," and he demonstrated their manifestation as seemingly universal archetypes in myths and universal human assumptions about the nature of reality.

In fact, through his study of womb and conception patterns he claimed to have discovered patterns that underlie and unite all of reality at all levels of manifestation — astronomical, social, personal, cellular, and even nuclear. While this may seem rather grandiose, his work was highly regarded and admired by Carl Jung.

Mott also carried forward the intimations of earlier prenatal theoreticians, notably Rank and Fodor, on the gestational basis of archetypes. While he does not address or seek to discredit the range of, supposedly genetic, archetypes postulated by Jung, his work is highly suggestive of an experiential, specifically, pre- and perinatal, as opposed to genetic basis for many of these.

## Denial and Incest Taboo

Mott (1960) also helped us to understand why if these prenatal memories are possible they are not more prevalent by suggesting denial is necessary in order to protect against incestuous feelings that might arise around feelings remembered from being inside one's mother.

## Devolutional Model of Consciousness Development

Finally, he made the postulation — hugely relevant to the theme of this work — that our original expanded capacity to feel is diminished, as he says, "divided," by experience not increased by it. The idea is that there is a reduction in awareness as a result of early traumatic events, beginning around conception and then on, and not the buildup of consciousness and feeling that we assume from the mechanistic paradigm that sees consciousness as a byproduct of increasing physical, specifically brain, activity during our early years.[1]

# Later Theorists — Breathwork

## Stanislav Grof

### Breathwork, LSD, Birth and Prenatal, Myth and Archetype, Spiritual and Consciousness

A pioneer in this prenatal area is Stanislav Grof (1976, 1980, 1985, 1990, to name a few). His many works, providing a framework for conceptualizing perinatal and transpersonal experiences, are a profound and useful starting point for an investigation into this area.

In his use of LSD beginning in 1956 for psychotherapy, called *psycholytic therapy*, he discovered four levels of experience of the unconscious: the *sensory*, the *biographical*, the *perinatal*, and the *transpersonal*. He noted a tendency for growth and healing to occur in a progressive way through these levels. The *sensory band* is the level of expanded sensory awareness and is usually initially encountered by participants. The *biographical band* is the realm of the personal unconscious wherein unintegrated and traumatic memories and material from childhood and one's personal history are retrieved, often relived, and integrated. The *perinatal* level of experience usually follows after dealing with the biographical material and involves the remembering, re-experiencing, and integrating of material that is related to the time prior to and surrounding birth. The *transpersonal band*, the level of spiritual experience, is usually reached after dealing with the other three levels.

### Four Modes of Experiencing — the Basic Perinatal Matrices

Grof has also delineated four matrices of experience, four general experiential constructs, which he called *basic perinatal matrices* (BPMs). He discovered that experiences at all levels of the unconscious often group themselves in four general ways that are roughly related to the four stages of birth. Thus, *Basic Perinatal*

*Matrix I* (*BPM I*) is related to the generally blissful or "oceanic" feelings that often characterize the fetus's state in the womb in early and middle pregnancy. *BPM II* is characterized by "no exit," hellish feelings that are related to the situation of the fetus in late pregnancy when the confines of the womb become ever more apparent but there is as yet no indication of any possibility of relief. *BPM III* relates to the birth process itself, the birth struggle, which is still characterized by feelings of compression and suffering but in which there is movement and change and thus hope of relief through struggle. If BPM II can be compared to hell, where there is no hope, BPM III is more like purgatory. Finally, *BPM IV* relates to the actual entry into the world, the termination of the birthing process, and is characterized by feelings of triumph, relief, and high, even manic, elation.

In his descriptions of the levels of experience and the matrices of perinatal experience, Grof has provided useful maps of the unconscious and experience in nonordinary states, which have incredible heuristic value in our understanding of cross-cultural religious and spiritual experience, psychopathology, personal growth, and consciousness and personality in general. And they have been utilized successfully in providing a context and guide for many tens of thousands of participants in his psycholytic and holotropic therapies.

However, while Grof is exhaustive in his descriptions of fetal and perinatal experience, he says less about the earlier experiences in the womb — the first trimester — and even less about conception and the experiences of sperm and egg — what is known as *cellular consciousness*. Still, this area is beginning to be discussed among his followers. And through his current nondrug modality, called *holotropic breathwork*, people are accessing these areas and beginning to give word to them (e.g., Carter, 1993).

# Frank Lake

## Breathwork, First Trimester, Early Experience as Foundation for Myths

Frank Lake, though less well-known again, has probably been the premier theoretician on the topic of prenatal events during the first three months of gestation. Just prior to his death in the early eighties, he wrote a culmination of his thirty-year investigation into pre- and perinatal influence in two works titled *Tight Corners in Pastoral Counselling* and *The First Trimester*. In these works he goes beyond his other works (for example, 1966) in placing the roots of all later experience, and in particular, distress, at the first three months of physical existence.

Lake began his investigation of re-experience in 1954. Like Stanislav Grof, he did this using LSD, initially, in the psycholytic therapy that was being developed at that time to facilitate therapeutic abreaction. Later he, again like Grof, developed a nondrug modality to accomplish the same thing. His method of "primal therapy" employed a type of fast breathing — again, like Grof's later technique — to access theta-wave brain levels, which are levels of consciousness that he saw as crucial to accessing and integrating these memories.

His thirty-year research led him to the realization of the importance of ever earlier experience. Thus his earlier stress on the importance of birth gave way to his later emphasis on the first trimester in 1981 (*Tight Corners in Pastoral Counselling*) and in 1982 (*The First Trimester*).

He stressed the *maternal-fetal distress syndrome*, beginning at around implantation, as a major time of trauma. He also described a blastocystic stage of relative bliss just prior to that.

His one other major disagreement with Grof was his belief that the mythological and symbolical elements described by Grof were a product of LSD and that the first trimester events were the actual roots of much of such symbolism and supposed transpersonal-mythological scenarios (1981, p. 35).

# Later Theorists — Myth and Sacred Text/Mysticism

## S. Giora Shoham

### Devolutional Model of Development, Falls from Grace

While not strictly a pre- and perinatal psychologist, I include this too little-known theoretician and criminologist because of the close relationship and influence his work has had upon my own work regarding these Falls from Grace. *Falls from Grace* and other devolutional models of consciousness postulate that during life and over time, beginning at conception, we actually are reduced in consciousness and awareness — not increased in it — and it corresponds to a "brain as reducing valve" theory of consciousness.[1]

While I initially constructed and wrote down my devolutional theory of consciousness — Falls from Grace — without the benefit of Shoham's work, upon discovering it I could not help but be both confirmed and reinspired by the astounding resonance his understanding has with my own.

Shoham (1979, 1990) starts his devolutional model in the womb and carries it through birth, weaning, and the oedipal periods of development. Though, as I delineate in Part 2, I disagree with his model by beginning mine at the creation of sperm and egg — as do other devolutional theorists like Francis Mott and David Wasdell — in virtually all other major instances his model corresponds to my own if one simply ... in keeping with a normal trend in child development in general as it begins to integrate the new pre- and perinatal evidence ... places everything back a little farther in time — in this case, specifically, one stage back.

# Later Prenatal Psychology Theorists — Cellular Memory and Conception, Foundations of Myth and Personality, Spirituality and Soul

## Lietaert Peerbolte

### Conception and Cellular Memory, Soul, Spirituality

Peerbolte (1954) was one of the earliest theorists to relate spirituality to conception and sperm/egg dynamics. In addition to claiming that a regression to conception is the inevitable result of all prenatal states, he traced the sense of "I" — the "I-function" — back to the egg, existing even in the mother's ovaries. He further postulated that the spiritual self was invisibly present within the field of attraction between the egg and the sperm. Correspondingly, he was the first to point out that the existence of conception, preconception, and even ovulation symbolism in dreams indicates the existence of a soul. For, he asked, what mind records these events otherwise?

I wrote the article, "A Primal Perspective on Spirituality," which was published in *The Journal of Humanistic Psychology* in 1985 and has now formed the basis for Section Two of this book, before I knew about Peerbolte's work. Yet, once again the conclusions I came to, especially about the existence of soul being established by the fact of these memories and especially those at the cellular levels of sperm and egg existence, are very much in line with his.

# Michael C. Irving

## Primal Therapy, Birth, Sperm, Egg, Myth, Dragon Symbolism, Prehistoric Cult and Ritual

Michael C. Irving is a primal therapist whose contributions include his relation of these earliest events from sperm and egg through the birth experience to fundamental mythological motifs and images across cultures. The originator of a way of interpretation that he calls *natalism*, he has brought together a host of artistic and artifactual images from a wide range of time periods and cultures which relate, with an astonishing degree of accuracy, to actual pre- and perinatal events.

In particular, he has traced the universal serpent/dragon motifs and mythology to birth and sperm experience, noting, among other things, that the serpent/dragon shape represents the birth canal or tunnel, that the fire-spewing characteristics of dragons relate to consuming pain, and that the constricting characteristics of snakes correspond to the constriction of the birth canal. Of great interest is his deduction that the widely prevalent snake and dragon cults, which were especially popular in prehistory, indicate an attempt to deal with such unfinished birth trauma material as we are only now, in modern times, rediscovering the importance of doing.

# Graham Farrant

## Primal Therapy; Sperm, Egg, Cellular Consciousness; Soul and Spirituality

Graham Farrant (1987; Buchheimer 1987), a psychiatrist and primal therapist from Australia, is probably the most influential and well-known of those discussing the phenomena that occur at the earliest times of our lives. In addition to echoing Lake in describing fetal, implantation, and blastocyst feelings, he has been able to elicit and describe sperm and egg imprints. He has found trauma from these earliest events to influence lifelong patterns of personality and behavior. He produced a notable video in which segments from the widely acclaimed movie "The Miracle of Life," which shows actual footage of gamete and zygote events, are juxtaposed via a split-screen with actual footage of a person reliving the exact same events in primal therapy — primal events which occurred before such cellular events were ever able to be seen and recorded. The effect is astounding in the detail in which the relivings replicate the actual cellular happenings.

In addition to his emphasis on cellular consciousness, Farrant has stressed the spiritual aspects of these earliest events. He relates incidents of spiritual trauma at the cellular level in which the individual splits off from Divinity — thus setting up a lifelong feeling of loss and yearning and a desire to return to Unity and the Divine.

# Paul Brenner

## Sperm, Egg, Cellular Consciousness and Biological Foundations of Myths

Paul Brenner (1991), a biologist and obstetrician, has presented at conferences and in workshops on the idea of the biological foundations of myth. For example, he relates basic biological, cellular events to biblical events described in *Genesis*.

He also relates male and female adult behavior to basic patterns of sperm and egg behavior and to events prior to and surrounding conception. He has said that male and female behavior are just sperm and egg activity grown up!

# Elizabeth Noble

## Cellular Consciousness and Spirituality, Empirical Underpinnings

Elizabeth Noble (1993) is an educator in the field of pregnancy and childbirth and is a student of Farrant's. She published a comprehensive overview of this new field, titled *Primal Connections*, in which she did not hesitate to stress the issues of cellular consciousness and the spirituality that appears to coincide with the re-experience of these earliest events. She provides empirical and theoretical avenues for understanding how memory can occur at such early times. Some of these are consistent with mainstream physicalist science; while others coincide with the cutting-edge, new-paradigm discoveries in fields such as biology, physics, and neuroscience.

# David Wasdell

## Sperm/Egg and First Trimester Imprints, Devolutional Model of Development, Social and Historical Implications

One of the more recent theoreticians in this area is David Wasdell. Wasdell's (1979, 1985a, 1985b, 1990) major contribution lies in his relating these earliest events to social and cultural patterns. He describes a process of devolution of consciousness beginning at around conception and proceeding through other reductions caused by traumas at implantation, in the womb, and at birth.

Most importantly, he delineates how the result of this diminution of potentiality is projected outwards into the problems and crises of violence, wars, and the mediocrity of modern personality on the scale of the masses and the macrocosms of the group, society, and global events.

In describing the problems of "normality" as rooted in a deprivational and deformational series of traumas from our earliest biological history, Wasdell emphasizes that this gives us the possibility to change that tragic social and personality outcome by focusing on the prevention and healing of such traumas. Thus, he holds out the vision of a new person and new society as an outcome of the efforts directed at the earliest laying down of human experience.

# 5

# The Importance of the Intrauterine for Understanding Our Times and the Goal of This Book

*This prenatal area in particular is ripe for reaping what it can teach us about what is human, about "human nature."*

Despite this long legacy of work and thought in this pre- and perinatal area, much of it, especially the prenatal, remains ignored by mainstream psychology and is largely unavailable to the public. Within the field itself, in addition, the prenatal information, in relation to the more widely accepted and circulated perinatal evidence, seems to be analogous to Otto Rank's (1929) ideas of birth trauma were to Sigmund Freud's concerning early infancy in that they are cast under an extra cloud of suspicion and disbelief and disregarded accordingly. Yet, like Rank's findings also, their main problem may lie with unfamiliarity and prejudice rather than validity or scientific viability; and these findings, like his were, may end up harkening the outlines of future endeavors and being confirmed by subsequent research.

Thus, I believe that this prenatal area in particular is ripe for reaping what it can teach us about what is human, about "human nature."

Therefore, *this book will put forth the possible relationship between our earliest ontogenetic experiences as humans and the structure of human consciousness and stages of human "development."*

I build a model that seeks an initial formulation of this information, teasing out its implications, and integrating it with relevant thinking and theoretical perspectives in anthropology, philosophy, psychology, and others.

However, before proceeding, it seems important to establish this pursuit within the logical-empirical framework that validates it. To do this, let us now turn to the re-experience movement I am most familiar with and feel to be the most important, primal therapy, and discuss its relation to the phenomenon of prenatal re-experience and spirituality.

# SECTION TWO

# THE LEGITIMACY OF PRENATAL SPIRITUALITY

# 6

How Valid Are Spiritual Experiences?
Psychedelic Research and Deep
Experiential Psychotherapy Have
Intensified the Exploration of Spiritual
Aspects of the Unconscious

*Primal Therapy: In Resolving Buried Tensions, One Sees
Clearly, Feels Freer, and Turns Cycles of Pain Into Cycles
of Joy*

The debate about the status we should ascribe to spiritual experience has been going on for a long time in psychology. Disagreement on this was crucial to Jung's break from Freud, with Jung postulating an unconscious containing transpersonal as well as purely personal elements.

More recently, LSD research and cathartic approaches to psychotherapy have extended the experiential exploration of spiritual aspects of the unconscious. Consequently, the legitimacy of spiritual experience has become an issue among some of us who primal.

Some of us who have been through primal therapy have begun to have experiences that we find difficult to trace to biological roots. But Janov, in his writings about primal, is consistent with the Freudian tradition in which he was tutored. He maintains a mechanistic interpretation of the primal process. He sees spiritual experiences as derivative of underlying primal pain and views meditation as "anti-Primal" (1970, p. 222).

For some who have continued primaling beyond Janov's prescribed limits, it is becoming apparent that he is unaware of some of the potentials of the process he presented. As one who began "feeling his feelings" over four decades ago, I will present an explanation of the relationship between the primal and spiritual processes as an alternative to Janov's mechanistic one.[1]

I rely on my own experiences, those I have observed in others in my role as facilitator and therapist, and the experiences of a number of other primalers as they have been related to me. I also rely on the important work with LSD and holotropic breathwork that Stanislav Grof (1970, 1976, 1980, 1985, 1988; Grof & Halifax, 1977; many more) has presented.

## Primal Therapy

It may be important to bring us up to date on primal therapy. Arthur Janov introduced it in 1970 with his controversial book, *The Primal Scream*, subtitled, *Primal Therapy: The Cure for Neurosis*. It had its time of ascendancy, with well-known personalities such as John Lennon espousing it. It also had a long period of malignment in print and the media, with much of the criticism apparently directed at Arthur Janov's style in presenting it or the excessive quality of his claims concerning it. Relevant articles, which were published in the *Journal of Humanistic Psychology*, are those by Kelley (1972), Kaufmann (1974), and Lonsbury (1978). Despite the controversy, however, primal therapy seems to have struck a chord in many people with its statement that the vast majority of us carry around a reservoir of unfelt pain from past experiences that was repressed because it was too overwhelming to be dealt with at the time. Primal therapy survived many of its contemporaries in the human potential movement.

Primal theory, simply stated, is that the memories of unfelt pain from traumatic experiences in childhood, at birth, and in the womb, and the emotions that would have naturally occurred with them, are locked in the body as unresolved tension. This tension motivates all neurotic and psychotic symptoms in its grosser manifestations, and in its subtler manifestations influences and shapes one's perceptions of and attitudes toward one's self and world, and thus determines one's behavior toward them. It does so in a manner that is symbolic of the unresolved need or trauma.

This pain/tension keeps us uncomfortable, keeps us from being able to see reality clearly and act positively, keeps us from being fully functioning, and keeps us forever viciously trapped in negative life situations that serve only to recreate the patterns of our past scars. In primal one opens up to these repressed memories and relives the traumatic events with all the emotion that should have been there, accompanying them, originally. In resolving the tensions, one sees more clearly and is able to act more positively and joyfully and to create more positive scenarios for one's life.

Space limits a complete description of primal theory or therapy, and for that I refer the reader to Janov and to the articles mentioned. That is, with a few modifications. Outside of Janov's own works, much of what has appeared in print has, as nearly as I can determine, been written by people who have neither been in nor been very close to primal therapy, the exception being Lonsbury (1978). In addition, little popular attention has been directed to it in recent years, and none to its development. I have been involved in a developing primal therapy and would like to amend the record accordingly.

I agree with much of what Kelley had to say in 1972. In Denver, where I did the majority of my therapy, the medical model was abandoned and an educational one was adopted, as per his suggestion. More importantly, Kelley noted the fallacy of a "postprimal" state, "cured" and devoid of defenses. That this state is an extrapolation of tendencies, as Kelley says, and the mythical qualities of a "primal man" as well as a "genital character," has become obvious to most of us who have been primaling for any extended period of time. To that extent, Kelley was well ahead of the rest of us in primal in seeing this. My major disagreement with his article is that it does not seem to take into account the deeper potentials of the primal process. He posits a need for an "education in purpose," which is separate from or "antithetical" to (an education in) feeling, and does not acknowledge the possible emergence of a "felt purpose," in the course of one's "feeling," that synthesizes the two.

But most of all, I feel it is important to respond to Kaufmann (1974). Much of his attitude and many of his assertions have been mirrored elsewhere in the media and have contributed to the prevailing distorted impression of primal that is at variance with what I will be describing. As other critics of primal have done, Kaufmann seems to have zeroed in on the excesses and inaccuracies of the early primal therapy as described in Janov's earliest works. A good example is his criticism of the "postprimal" person. This indolent, sexless character has been the source of much confusion and disdain for primal therapy. And Kaufmann's remarks clearly are admissible considering the date. But let me say emphatically that this particular notion of a "real person" was later abandoned both in the publications coming out of Janov's Primal Institute ("A connected person achieves."[2]) and among us primalers. We just didn't turn out that way.

Janov's early characterization began to be seen as someone just on the verge of making a more precipitous descent into earlier, "first-line," preverbal feelings.

Other of the early inaccuracies eventually were cleared up in practice. The primal therapy I experienced in Denver in 1975 with Jules and Helen Roth and their staff was an evolved version of primal as originally described by Janov (1970), or as initially presented to me in Toronto by Thomas Verny in 1972. It was less directive, more supportive. We did not maintain the illusion (as much) that anyone could really know where someone else was "at" and so we did not pretend that we could "bust" each other. Similarly, we did not use "props" or attempt to interpret one another's experiences. We let one another "be" more fully where we already were and helped one another to go "deeper." I specify the discrepancies because they relate to what I say further on.

I might also add that while in Denver I was witness and participant in primal's continued development. Initially, it did contain many elements of a "primal religion" as often criticized. Subsequently, we let go of illusions of that nature and were able to integrate this invaluable tool into a fuller life and into a broader framework of understanding. My impression from other primalers is that similar evolutions occurred elsewhere.

The point I make is that the primal therapy to which I refer is quite unlike the popular notions of "primal scream therapy" and different in many ways from its earliest descriptions. My response to detractors of early primal therapy is just that many of their criticisms are no longer relevant.

# 7

# Is God a Defense? Is Passion Not Spiritual? To Travel Unafraid Through All the Rooms of One's House

*Stopping the "Internal Dialogue": Meditation and Primal*
*Are Attempts to Experience Aspects of Consciousness That*
*Are Nonverbal, Noncortical, and Non-Neurotic*

## Is God a Defense?

This section is part of the development in primal in correcting one inaccuracy of the early "primal scream," which is Janov's attitude regarding the relation between feeling one's feelings and the spiritual process. Janov would claim that religion and the belief in a God are defenses, and that spiritual experiences employ the energy of repressed material, as in sublimation, or are reaction formations to such pain. Specifically, Janov has stated that meditation is "anti-Primal."

### Is Catharsis Anti-Spiritual?

Attacking from the other side we have Wilber (1982) claiming that preverbal experiences are to be distinguished from transpersonal experiences. He claims that "because both pre-X and trans-X are, in their own ways, non-X, they may appear similar, even identical, to the untutored eye," whereas in reality they are profoundly different (p. 5). He posits a structure of linear development in which one conceivably could "regress" to pre-X, to prepersonal experience, and mistake it for transpersonal experience.

Therefore he would claim that such experiences as we undergo in the phenomenon of re-experience are actual "regressions" on the spiritual path and are antithetical to a true spiritual quest. He would also claim a spiritual meditative practice is antithetical to one of re-experience or "regression therapy."

# Meditation Is Often Emotionally "Messy"

Wilber's theory strikes me as a curiously dualistic way of interpreting a nondichotomous reality. And although his reasoning is tight and internally consistent, it excludes the evidence of transpersonal experience as exhibited in the spiritual, psychedelic, and ethnographic literature, as well as the evidence of meditation research. For, as Epstein and Leiff, (1981, p. 140) wrote in commenting on Wilber's distinctions between supposed pre- and transpersonal experience: "In fact, meditation experiences embody all of the above. Confusion arises when meditation is analyzed as one discrete state, rather than as a developmental process."

### Spiritual Growth Is Not a Linear Path, It Is an Expanding Outward

Thus, I differ with Wilber in that I do not see pre-egoic influences as counter to a transcendental path; rather, I see them as distortions to be worked through.

This stems from the basic difference between our developmental frameworks in that Wilber sees a linearity, and I see a dialectic in which a transcendental jump "forward" may require an incorporative "backward" step. I do not see growth at all as a linear progression, but more like an expanding outward.

## To Travel Unafraid Through All the Rooms of One's House

What we find, in primal anyway, is that one actually is more adult when one can let one's self be childlike at times. Wilber's theory seems to exclude the possibility that the "healthiest" state may be, as many have described it, one in which we have access all the way "up" and "down" the "spectrum," in which we can travel unafraid through all the rooms of our house. In this context *regression* can seem a meaningless term and discussion of it appear spurious.

# An Alternative Explanation

Thus, unlike Janov who casts a dark light on spiritual pursuits in affirming the importance of primal experience (re-experience), Wilber impugns the validity of "pre-" experiences (re-experience) in affirming the importance of spiritual and meditative experiences.

## Regression Is the Left Hand of Progression

My purpose here will be to counter both theorists in affirming that "pre-" is not distinct from "trans-," as Wilber stated, nor primal distinct from meditation, as Janov stated.

Basically, the evolved primal therapy I participated in differs with Janov in discovering that primal and meditation are congruent techniques beneath their surface differences. This is evident in the similarity of the phenomena experienced in each and in the similarity of effects each has on the personality.

Their congruence is further indicated by the fact that transpersonal phenomena do seem to occur to advanced primalers, contrary to Janov's claims. Though experiences of both primalers and LSD subjects seem to indicate that much of what is generally considered transpersonal phenomena is derivative of traumatic life experiences, particularly those occurring at birth or in the womb, there is much of transpersonal experience that cannot be explained away in that manner.

## Stopping the "Internal Dialogue"

The alternative explanation I am presenting rests on the idea that the purpose of the spiritual disciplines is, as Castaneda has termed it, to stop the "internal dialogue." This corresponds in primal therapy to the attempts to get "below" the rationalizations, intellectualizations, and defenses that are laid down in the cortex, to the real body feelings underneath. It would seem that both methods are engaged in an attempt to delve into and experience aspects of consciousness that are nonverbal, nonsymbolic, noncortical, and nonneurotic.

Neurosis has often been defined as a narrowing of consciousness. One way of viewing this is that it entails being cut off from large areas of awareness and experience that are tied up with painful memories and feelings. In this light it is interesting to consider a statement by Paramahansa Yogananda, who was discussing his experience of returning to a physical body in his reincarnation on earth. He writes, "Like a prodigal child, I had run away from my macrocosmic home and imprisoned myself in a narrow microcosm" (1946, p. 168).

## "Imprisoned in a Narrow Microcosm" = Human

One way of viewing the human condition, then, is as a "neurotic" state in that it entails a narrowing of consciousness. We see neurosis in the pathological sense as simply a more extreme narrowing of consciousness than what is accepted as normal.

In this way we can see the function of the spiritual disciplines, which is to increase the capacity of the individual to accept the "larger reality," as parallel to the purpose of primal therapy, which is to increase the capacity of the person to accept walled-off portions of her or his personal reality. As they apparently deal with different "levels" of reality, one might suspect that there would be differences in technique.

## Catharsis and Calmness Alternate on Liberation's Highway

But, conversely, I propose that primal and spiritual techniques are complementary, despite their surface differences, with either being helpful depending on the material to be worked through. Further and more specifically, I propose that primal can aid the spiritual process by clearing out negative material from the personal unconscious that would otherwise distort and impede that process, whereas spiritual techniques sometimes can be helpful in extending the arena of growth beyond the borders of strictly primal (or personal) reality.

# 8

# Cathartic Meditation: "At Times I Hopped Like a Frog … Between Smiles and Tears, I Continued my Inward Journey" — Guru Muktananda

*The Path Is Different from the Goal: The Truth About Meditation Can Only Now Be Told — Real Meditation Is About Letting Go and Experiencing Not About Controlling Oneself*

## What *Really* Happens in Authentic, Deep Meditation

Janov's position that meditation is simply an attempt at inducing relaxation, which is then called bliss and couched in terms like "oneness with God" (1970, pp. 221-222), is an uninformed opinion that leaves out of consideration the variety of spiritual experiences that occur during meditation.

## Only Now Can It Be Told

It is understandable why Janov might think this, however. Explicit information on meditation experiences, especially during the earliest stages, has not always been easy to come by. For centuries there existed the belief that spiritual experiences were to be kept secret and not freely discussed. But the belief that emerges in our age is that the times are such as to make possible certain allowances that formerly were denied. In this vein several masters have in this century written personal accounts of their spiritual experiences; some even have allowed themselves to be tested by scientific methods. Adding to this are the findings of the ever increasing body of meditation research that, for the first time in history, has been taking place in the last half century.

# Cathartic Meditation

"Between Smiles and Tears, I Continued my Inward Journey." — Guru Muktananda

From the writings of Paramahansa Yogananda (1946) and Swami Baba Muktananda (1974), we are able to derive a conception of meditational experiences that is totally at variance with the notion that it is merely an attempt at relaxation or that it is, as Wilber claimed, distinct from "pre-" states. Muktananda writes, for example, "Various feelings emerged during meditation," and "Sometimes I was happy, sometimes sad. Alternating between smiles and tears, I continued my inward journey" (p. 75).

He talks about innumerable movements that occur in the process of meditation (p. 77). Most interestingly, he notes that these movements are automatic and "continued for a prolonged period" (pp. 82-83). "At times I hopped like a frog. Occasionally my body moved violently as if possessed by a spirit" (p. 78).

## The Yogic Experiences No One Tells You About

Muktananda explains that "the practitioners of Siddha Yoga have a vast variety of experiences about which one neither hears nor reads" (p. 76); that because of this an aspirant might abandon the path out of sheer fright (p. 77). Unaware of the variety of emotions and experiences entailed in the spiritual process, expecting perhaps only "bliss" (or relaxation?), the aspirant may think he or she is going insane (p. 77). He himself, however, sees all these experiences as part of a natural process that is cleansing in nature and makes possible access to higher levels of consciousness.

## "Meditators Commonly Experienced Intense Feeling States...."

Additional examples of these kinds of meditational experiences are given by Kapleau (1980) and Kornfield (1979). In fact, Kornfield reports that incidences of "spontaneous movement" were the most common experiences reported by beginning meditators (p. 45). He notes also that "Meditators commonly experienced intense feeling states and frequent dramatic changes of mood," with examples of such including "screaming mind trips," "violent crying," "huge release of anger," and "heavy sadness" (pp. 47-48).

# The Goal Is Different from the Path

In these descriptions of emotional discharge/release we can see similarities to what is described as occurring in primal therapy.

## Spontaneous, Automatic Movement in Meditation ~ First-Line Feelings in Primal Therapy

But the descriptions of spontaneous and automatic movement are especially interesting. In many respects they recall the experiences that primalers with access to their "first-line" pain (preverbal, usually surrounding birth) frequently encounter. In fact, it is exactly this kind of relation (between the physical and emotional experiences reported by Kapleau, Kornfield, and others and perinatal experiences occurring outside of the spiritual disciplines) that is noted by Bache (1981).

The bliss and equanimity described in the spiritual literature are thus associated most strongly with the advanced stages of meditation and should not be confused with the experiences entailed in the process of getting there.

## Most of What Passes for Meditation Is Anything But Mystical

The point is that there is more to meditation than mere relaxation or undiluted "trans-" states. Although evidently, as Rowan (1983) put it, "Most of what passes for meditation has nothing much to do with mystical experiences at all — it is just the achievement of a very calm state" (p. 21). From what I have seen, most of meditation as understood today is about learning to become more repressed and neurotic ... less alive. It is all about trying to push out of consciousness all the upsetting things of life — all the things which when faced, embraced, and integrated can be gone beyond and can enrich one.

Still, Rowan continues, "it is possible to get small or large peak experiences through meditation" (p. 21).

## Real Meditative Experience May Not Be So Relaxing

Thus, it appears that the techniques of relaxation have to do with attempting to still the vagaries of pain-derived tension, the internal dialogue, so as to gain access to areas of consciousness that are "outside" and more fundamental than these vagaries. And contact with those areas may not be so relaxing!

# 9

# The Primal Serene: How Passion Promotes Serenity and the Detached Observer in Catharsis — The Eye of the Storm

*Catharsis Makes Us Aware, by Contrast, of a Strong,*
*Unaffected Self Within ... Catharsis and Calmness: We*
*Gain Insight Into the Illusion of Maya and Rootedness in a*
*Deeper Self*

## The Primal Serene

This technique of meditation — the stilling of the internal cacophony — is in some ways exactly opposite to primal ones. Primal involves the "tossing out" of all the vagaries — the manifesting in a verbal or physical way of the tensions existing in the body at the moment. But the results of each appear the same. Characteristically, following a primal one finds oneself sinking into a serene and markedly relaxed state. It appears that spiritual techniques differ from primal in attempting to reach that state directly by conscious control over the body/mind. Once that state is reached, it allows further abatement of physiological processes and, hence, access to even subtler realms of consciousness.

A primaler also can be viewed as open to subtler energies after having reached a "cleared out" relaxed state via primaling, and could conceivably use a technique like meditation to increase that access.

I was surprised to discover, after originally proposing this relation between catharsis and meditation in 1979 and approaching from the stance of psychotherapy, that Bhagwan Shree Rajneesh had already made the same kind of formulation coming at it from the spiritual perspective. It is described in his book, *Meditation: The Art of Ecstasy* (1976). See especially the chapter on "Chaotic Meditation."

At any rate, Primal or a similar deep experiential psychotherapy then becomes a method of dealing with the grosser manifestations of psychobiological energy that keep the body in a tense and overdetermined state. Once these energies are dealt with and released, it becomes possible to employ a "mindfulness" type of meditation to deal with subtler energies, to connect with and dissipate those subtler energies, and thereby to gain access to subtler energies still.

# The Detached Observer in Catharsis — The Eye of the Storm

Another way to look at the relation between catharsis and calmness, and the benefits that one can have for the other, is suggested by Heider (1974). He points out in his article, "Catharsis in Human Potential Encounter," that "as a rule the person actually going through catharsis reports no feelings of fear even at times when he appeared most fearful; it is as if there is a detached observer who knows that the process is natural and even necessary" (p. 37). Indeed, one can let go into extreme emotional states time and time again and remain always aware of the "detached observer" part of oneself.

A major benefit of catharsis is that as this continually happens one becomes increasingly conscious of a part that is unaffected by the turmoil — the part that is there, observing at the onset of agitation, that "sits quietly by" watching in the midst of catharsis, and that is there to silently aid one through "reentry" and into the calm state afterward.

Thus, catharsis makes us distinctly aware, through contrast, of a strong, silent, unaffected self within; it makes us aware of an "unchanging" that contrasts with all the violent changingness. In so doing it helps us to be more in contact with that self and its subtler pushes, pulls, and impulses — its subtler pattern. We become increasingly aware of a more fundamental self that is unmoved by all the chaos of consciousness.

To that extent, it corresponds to those phases of meditation that entail the encounter with disruptive material with the admonition not to get caught up in them, to refuse them energy by believing in them.

Indeed this attitude can be the result of catharsis. We can release the explosive energy born of "attachment," in the Buddhist sense, and hence gain insight into the illusion of "maya," the fleeting changingness, and gain rootedness in a more inviolable self.

# 10

## Approaching the "Source": Right-Left Brain Integration; Theta Waves ... Hypnogogic Experiences; and Delta Waves ... A Nightly Return to Our Roots in the Infinite

*The Awareness of a "Larger Reality": Brain Correlates to Primal and Spiritual Experience ... Wave and Structure*

## Brain Waves

The relations between these levels of growth and the techniques under consideration can be demonstrated by their correlations with brain wave activity.

Theta Waves ... Hypnogogic Experiences

Beta waves on the EEG correspond to normal waking consciousness while alpha indicates a more relaxed, tranquil state.

The consciousness correlated with theta waves, which are even slower than alpha, is characterized by a dream-like or "reverie" state during which one is immersed in a world of images. It has long been known that these dream-like states (called "hypnogogic experiences") play some part in scientific and artistic creation. (Rama, Ballentine, & Ajaya, 1976, pp. 146-147)

## Delta Waves — A Nightly Return to Our Roots in the Infinite

An even more relaxed state is the delta state, which usually is only experienced in the phase of "deep sleep." It is unknown what exactly goes on during this state of sleep as, unlike REM sleep, which is characterized by dreaming, this appears to be a dreamless state. Yogananda (1946, p. 493) has indicated that it represents a nightly return to our roots in the infinite. Regardless, it is a more relaxed state than even the very relaxed and creative theta state.

Theta has been called a measure of feeling states by Janov (1974b, p. 40). He also has brought forth research showing a trend toward theta and delta states in advanced primalers (cf. Janov & Holden, 1975, p. 493; Janov, 1971, pp. 214-215). Lake (1981) also makes this connection between theta states and integrative primal access and relivings. Similarly, research on meditators has indicated that they also exhibit alpha, theta, and delta wave patterns while awake, with more advanced meditators exhibiting the slower brain-wave patterns (cf. Rama et al., 1976, pp. 159-161; Walsh, 1979, p. 166).

## The Awareness of a "Larger Reality"

We see that at least in regard to brain-wave activity the effects of primal and meditation are parallel. The effects include increasingly relaxed patterns and greater synchronization. One might speculate that the correlate of these slower rhythms is the awareness of subtler and subtler energies (a primaler would say "feelings"). These energies and awarenesses are unavailable in the normal beta state and could therefore be said to represent the awareness of a "larger reality."

# Brain Structure

In addition to brain-wave activity, one might also find correlates to this process in terms of actual parts of the brain.

## Right Brain — Left Brain Integration

Much has been made correlating states of consciousness and areas of the brain along right brain/left brain lines. Left brain dominance has come under attack and an integration of the two is called for. It is becoming clear that this kind of integration is an important aspect of both the primal and spiritual processes. Evidence for this is presented by Janov (1973; Janov & Holden, 1975). And evidence of this kind of integration occurs in the spiritual disciplines, particularly in its most advanced stages (Earle, 1981).

## Approaching the "Source"

What I am saying is that contact with subtler energies may involve awareness of brain activity existing closer to the brainstem, the "source" of brain activity, while normal consciousness is awareness of brain activity that is primarily cortical. Both the much acclaimed ability of yogis to control physiological processes that normally are unconsciously regulated and the reports that primalers are more aware of internal biological processes attest to this conception of the process.

# 11

# Levels of Pain, Levels of Bliss, and the First Shutdown: "I Went from Birth to an Intrauterine State to Conception to Floating in the Icy Vastness of Space."

*Experiences of Overwhelming Energy and Joy Have Been Described: Four Levels of Psychedelic Experience and a Primal Spirituality*

## LSD Therapy

The strongest support for the alternative explanation, however, comes from research done by Stanislav Grof with LSD. Grof has described the reliving of traumatic experiences from childhood, birth, and in the womb, of people under the influence of LSD, that seem almost identical to experiences described by primalers.[3]

## Four Levels of Deep, Psychedelic Experience

Grof delineates four levels of the drug state, each deeper than the preceding one: the aesthetic, the psychodynamic, the perinatal, and the transpersonal. These also represent a progression in that the usual course, over a series of LSD sessions, is to go beyond the initial levels, after having experienced and resolved the particular tasks/problems on those levels (1970, pp. 19-20). Consequently, the transpersonal level is only reached by persons in advanced stages of LSD therapy.

The psychodynamic and perinatal level experiences, although containing additional symbolic elements not always found in the primal process, show striking similarities to experiences of what Janov has termed "second-line" and "first-line" pain.

## Levels of Primal Experience, Levels of Pain

*First-line pain* is preverbal. It relates to traumatic experiences that occurred *en utero*, at birth, and for a period of about six months after birth. There is a life and death urgency about these kinds of feelings, relating as they do to a time of complete helplessness and dependence on others and an inability to separate one's self from painful experience by conceptualizing it. This kind of pain often relates to matters of biological necessity, and the memories of the traumatic experiences are registered in subcortical parts of the brain. First-line appears to be identical to Grof's perinatal level of the unconscious.

*Second-line pain* is more verbal and relates to traumatic or hurtful events from childhood, after the child has begun to use concepts to structure his or her experience. The memories associated with this level are more accessible to consciousness, registered, as they are, in the cortex. Second-line appears to be identical to Grof's psychodynamic or biographical level.

## Levels of Pain, Levels of Bliss

The manner in which these levels are experienced, the progression from later and more accessible to earlier and deeper, the way that the pains are resolved, and the manner in which unresolved pains influence postsession intervals — all seem to be similar and often identical in the primal and the LSD experiences.

However, one striking difference exists. Beyond the "primal" levels of the LSD experience, Grof has described experiences of a transpersonal nature that do not appear to have any roots in the personal pain of the participant and appear to be experiences *sui generis*. The experiences on this level are incredibly varied and range from past-incarnation experiences to ancestral memories, certain kinds of archetypal experiences, and, on what appears to be its most profound level, consciousness of "Universal Mind" and "Metacosmic Void."

# Primal-Spiritual Feelings

The question naturally arises as to why primalers who are able to experience psychodynamic and perinatal phenomena without drugs are not reported to be contacting feelings of a transpersonal nature. Contrary to Janov's published reports, there are some indications of it occurring. Some long-term primalers with whom I have contact have talked of receiving love, helping, strength, or bliss that seemed to be coming from a place beyond the scope of their current physical existence, to be emanating from a "higher power" of some sort. Their descriptions have many parallels to some descriptions of spiritual experience.

## "I Was Three Things: Sperm, Egg, and a Cosmic Life Force."

Experiences of overwhelming energy and joy have been described. One person used the terms "cosmic life force," "cosmic energy," and "God power" to describe his experience. He remarked that it was of such intensity that it would have been too much to experience at an earlier stage in his therapy and related it to a time before he was conceived. He said that he had the realization that "I was three things: sperm, egg, and a cosmic life force."

Another primaler, Belden Johnson (1991) described his experience:

*In a sort of sped-up time-lapse film that ran quickly backwards, I went from birth to an intrauterine state to conception to floating in the icy vastness of space, surrounded by the faint light pricks of distant stars. At first my Observer-mind came in with, "Hm. Symbolic ideation. The soul floating in space between embodiments and all that."*

But he quickly changed his diagnosis:

*"Nope. You're a tiny part of the whole shtick , old boy. An atom in space, a mote of consciousness, a tiny fragment of the God head." (p. 54)*

## The First Shutdown

It is no coincidence that these last two experiences revolve around conception and cellular consciousness. Indeed, our sense is that these spiritual experiences often are related to gaining access to a time before the first "shutdown," which is the first time that trauma forces a retreat from one's full capabilities and consciousness. Our experience has been that the time before initial shutdown varies among people, but usually ranges from before the fertilization of the egg to some time *en utero*.

Exactly when and how this shutdown occurs will be the major theme of the rest of this book, *Falls from Grace*. While the time of major shutdown appears to vary, shutting down or retreat from full capabilities appears to happen gradually, and in stages — with earlier access correlating with relatively more spiritual, transpersonal access.

# 12

# The Roots of Bliss: The Joy Beneath the Pain and Positive Possibilities of Experiential Process

*Spiritual Experiences Occur in Deep Therapy: Helping Entities, Past-Incarnations, Satori, Synchronicity, Inner Guidance, Life Force, Archetypes, and the Collective Unconscious*

## Transpersonal, Spiritual Experiences Occurring in Deep Experiential Psychotherapy

On the more exotic side, experiences of which I am aware that have had a transpersonal quality to them include encounters with and messages from "helping entity" types and infusions of colored "helping energy." Experiences that have had past-incarnation qualities also have been reported, but they apparently occur only when they are important for the individual's understanding or resolution of her or his present concerns. All of the experiences I am reporting occurred to people who had been primaling for a minimum of four years, working through birth and womb material much of that time.

## Parallel to the Effects of Long-Term Spiritual Practice

In addition to these reports of experiences had in or through primaling, we note gains in equanimity similar to those described for meditators and the occurrence of satori-like states. Cleared of attachment to the past and the future strivings that come of it, experiences with a marked sense of "nowness" are common. Corresponding elements of synchronicity between inner and outer states, effortless doing, and inner guidance appear also, correlates for which seem primarily to be associated with the effects of long-term spiritual practice.

# The Joy Beneath the Pain

## Archetypes and the Collective Unconscious

Finally, we might note that there are some primalers who are reported to experience phenomena described as archetypal and related to the collective unconscious (McCloud, 1975). McCloud uses the terms "transpersonal" and "mystical" to describe the quality of the experiences inherent in contact with this area of the unconscious. He says that these experiences can occur during the state of "total physical calm" that follows the "period of high physical activity or agitation" characteristic of "direct encounter with the negative and fearful aspects of the Unconscious" (p. 288). McCloud claims that experiences during these "deep inner meditative states" may take the form of "a spontaneous (noncortical) flow of images through the mind or, especially in more advanced persons . . . may consist of what seems afterward to have been a total void" (p. 289).

# One Must Discover One's Own Truth

McCloud contends that since Janov's framework does not include such experiences, these unfamiliar and nonrational experiences are forced into the familiar primal paradigms. These primal rationalizations then become a defense at the point at which deeper experiences are possible, thus preventing the full experience of these deeper levels. Interestingly, McCloud also claims that what is helpful in experiencing these levels is to be given "support but little or no direction" (p. 284), in strong contrast to Janov's directive techniques. One might conclude from this that different experiences and different interpretations are possible when one is allowed to discover one's own "truth" as opposed to a preconceived one.

# Joyful Possibilities of Experiential Process

Anyway, as far as the "blissful" experiences mentioned, it appears that the reason we hear little of them in regard to primal therapy is because Janov himself has been unaware of the joyful possibilities of the primal process. As Lonsbury (1978) points out, Janov's is an incomplete theory of feeling based only on feeling "Pain": All else is labeled "crazy." Also Janov specifically states that the goal of primal is not "happiness" (1970, p. 101), which he sees as a neurotic state (1972, pp. 164-172) but, rather, something like "contentment" (p. 168). He sees primal people as "scarred" people who are able to use primal to better their life situation from the horror that it otherwise would be (1970, p. 136). His use of the word "contentment" leads me to suspect that he is talking about a state of reduced tension following abreaction (cf. 1970, p. 102; 1972, p. 218).

## The Roots of Bliss

The fact is that not only are advanced primalers dipping into areas more akin to bliss than mere contentment, but Grof also, through his LSD research, has demonstrated the existence of positive and joyful experiences existing alongside the negative ones at the deep perinatal level of the psyche. Grof gives these "positive COEX systems" the same status as the "negative COEX systems," which is his term for the traumatic experiences laid down in the brain needing to be relived. Grof claims that positive COEX systems relate to particularly blissful experiences from one's personal life, having their deepest roots in blissful intrauterine and postnatal experiences.

## Bliss and the Womb

The fact that Janov does not seem to know about these positive potentials of the primal process seems to be related to his disregard of womb experiences. Although both LSD subjects and advanced primalers outside of Janov's Primal Institute have often described embryonal experiences, down even to the sperm and egg level, Janov has little to say about womb experiences in his writings and considers sperm experience a fantasy (1974a, p. 323). That some of the positive experiences mentioned do not begin to happen until one has felt back to those levels, then, would help to explain his ignorance of them.

Through my own experiences with spiritual disciplines and primal I have come to believe that the bliss the yogis and meditators describe is the same as the "alive" or "life force" feelings described by primalers. Contrary to Janov's assertion, I believe it is an error to describe this state of "spiritual" bliss as a state of being totally cut off from one's body, as "anti-Primal." Primalers describe the feeling of being cut off with words like "deadness" or "numbness," never "bliss."

# 13

# The Making of a Calmer Crazy Person … Why Meditation by Itself Is Often Not Enough: Non-Conceptual Experience

*Cerebral Distortion and the Importance of Connection: It May Be That, Without Therapy, the Real Benefits of Spiritual Practice Are Not Attainable by Most Westerners*

## Non-Conceptual Experience

It would seem that some spiritual disciplines and religions are able to give some people a taste of more "alive" experiences than would ordinarily be possible by temporarily reducing the amount of pain-energized cortical activity or "noise." In Huxley's classic work, *The Doors of Perception* (1954), he makes a point that there are many "temporary by-passes" to "brain-as-reducing-valve," some of which he directly relates to a slowdown of cortical activity through physiological means (pp. 23-24).

## Meditation Tries to "Cut Through" the Pain

Meditation, specifically, appears to be a method of attempting to still the pain-driven cortical ramblings to gain access to nonverbal experience. In primal terms it may be said to be an attempt to bypass second-line pain and go directly to nonconceptual first-line material. This is not to say that some second-line is not dealt with. In addition to the evidence presented by Kornfield (1979) and Kapleau (1980), we might also remember that Muktananda's journey inward was characterized by smiles *and* tears. Apparently, some second-line connections were made. Yet the meditative technique seems structured, basically, to get "below" these "personal" levels as soon as possible.

In meditation one attempts to maintain a "calm, detached attitude while observing his mental processes," and the goal is to attend to thoughts that will deepen meditation and allow other distracting or disturbing thoughts to arise and burst without becoming involved in them (Rama et al., 1976, pp. 149-150). In this way the body learns to associate the relaxed state with what had formerly been disturbing thoughts, ever productive of cerebral "noise."

## Primal and Meditation Both Access Nonconceptual Experience

This meditation technique is vastly different from a primal one wherein all disturbing thoughts are allowed full sway in consciousness. Nevertheless, both do seem to provide access to underlying nonverbal levels. In fact, I have been told by one person who has experienced first-line pain in both meditation and primal that the phenomena encountered are identical: They are primarily body phenomena that the conceptual parts of the brain can interpret in a number of ways.

## Meditation and Primal Both Access Body Memories of Birth and the Perinatal

In this respect, we might recall the descriptions of death-rebirth that are so commonly found in the spiritual literature and in the ethnographies of nonliterate peoples. Though primalers will invariably relate their particular experiences of this sort to their own biological births, in the psychedelic literature we find many examples of people reliving their births and using spiritual concepts, such as death-rebirth, to explain their experiences ... although it should be noted that often in subsequent relivings the biological elements become too obvious to ignore.

## The Importance of Connection

Apparently, it is only in the ways that these experiences are interpreted that shows up as a difference between them. Whereas Muktananda felt the "hopping" his body did was like that of a frog, someone in primal might realize that the jerks and kicks were actually the eruption of unresolved tensions from her or his birth.

Janov would say, however, that this difference in interpretation is an important one. For if one is interpreting these nonverbal body feelings in spiritual or other terms, one is not linking them up with one's personal reality or one's own experiences. One is not "connecting"; one is not seeing how that particular pattern of pain has influenced one's second-line pain, nor how it has influenced one's life history and present patterns of behavior. Thus, Janov would say that no change in those patterns of behavior can occur.

## Cerebral Distortion

It would seem that first-line access without connection to second- and third-line — that is to say, without connection to how those birth and prenatal events influenced one's childhood experiences and current life feelings and circumstances — would keep the cortical programs intact. Neural energies would continue proceeding along familiar distorted pathways, and these pain-necessitated elements of the antiquated defense system would remain to influence and distort the perceptions of one's deeper experiences.

## A Calmer State with a Disturbed Understanding May Result from Meditation on Its Own

On the other hand, one could make a case that very real, repressed energy is released during these first-line encounters no matter how they are interpreted. This energy, then, is no longer driving the excess cortical activity common to neurotics and characteristic of the beta state. The effect is that of less "noise," calmer brain wave activity, and an increased capability to gain access to subtler energies.

Therefore, the fact that connections are not made and the original cerebral pathways are not altered seems to mark the difference between the primal and spiritual first-line encounters. I will discuss the effects of this further on.

# Differences in Pain

It should be pointed out that for some this difference may not represent a real problem. Some people may simply not have much second-line pain, or even first-line pain blocking the perception of clear Reality.

## People Differ in the Amount of Life Trauma Separating Them from Bliss

Apparently, there are vast differences in the amount of pain that people carry around, as Grof has demonstrated in reference to his LSD subjects. He found that there were some people who, after dealing with and reliving psychodynamic and perinatal material for a few sessions, would proceed to transpersonal experiences for the remainder of their sessions. This was especially true of professionals who were undergoing the treatment as part of their training. This was in contrast to others with manifest neurotic and psychotic symptoms, many of whom had been hospitalized and often required scores of sessions dealing with their personal material before proceeding to transpersonal material (Grof, 1970, p. 2).

# 14

# Karmic Genetics: Bad Karma Enters Us Through Our Birth and Womb Experiences … Meditation as a Defense

*"Pranic Lifetrons in the Spermatazoa and Ova … Guide …
the Embryo According to a Karmic Design": Defusing
Mental Contortions … Aiding Meditation*

## "Humanity … Is Neurotic."

Also there might be cultural differences. Bhagwan Shree Rajneesh (Osho) wrote that "humanity, itself, is neurotic" because society requires that each person be "conditioned" and "molded into a particular pattern" and not be "allowed to be just whatever he is" (1976, p. 26). Further, he said that this may have had something to do with the fact that the great spiritual masters, who themselves realized, could not help the greater portion of humanity to reach enlightenment (p. 27).

## Westerners Might Be "Crazier" and Thus Find It More Difficult

Keep this in mind along with the evidence that Americans have traditionally ranked among the lowest in the world in the general indulgence we afford our infants (Whiting & Child, 1953). Additionally, we are, in cross-cultural perspective, "quite severe in the general socialization of [our] children," especially in regards to such important events as weaning and toilet training where we have been judged to be "exceptionally early and exceptionally severe" and "in a hurry to start the training process" (p. 320). These things being true, we may say that we are, in some ways, more "neurotic" than many other cultures.

## It May Be That the Real Benefits of Spiritual Practice Cannot Be Gained by Most Westerners

Considering all this we might question why we think we can just adopt, wholesale, the techniques that have been developed down through the centuries and, especially, for use in other cultures. For if, as Rajneesh says, the spiritual techniques do not work because they do not address humanity as it is — that is to say, neurotic — then meditation and similar practices may be said to be even less applicable to a modern "severely conditioned" … and more traumatized … Westerner.

## Demons Lacking in the Liberated

In this same vein, it is interesting how often yogis and spiritual masters speak of having had uneventful childhoods and loving parents. Paramahansa Yogananda mentions this in respect to his childhood. And it is not inconceivable that this may have had something to do with the seeming lack of "demons" with which he had to contend and with the exceptionally blissful, beautiful, and loving perception of the infinite that he presents in his autobiography.

# Bad Karma Enters Us Through Our Prenatal and Perinatal Traumas

The spiritual explanation for these differences in levels of primal pain has been that the yogi-to-be has worked through most of his or her karma in previous lifetimes, and that there is a link between karmic influences and the "life situation" to which one returns, which would include the amount of first- and second-line pain to which one is subjected. This notion of a link between karmic influences and one's "life situation" is not found only in the spiritual literature. For example, Grof (1976) notes that LSD experiences of previous incarnations sometimes occur alongside experiences involving the reliving of disturbances of intrauterine life (pp. 108-109). In discussing the experiences of one such subject, he writes as follows:

*He was . . . experiencing episodes that appeared to be past-incarnation memories. It seemed as if elements of bad karma entered his present life in the form of disturbances of his embryonal existence and as negative experiences during the period he was nursed. He saw the experiences of the "bad womb" and "bad breast" as transformation points between the realm of the karmic law and the phenomenal world governed by natural laws as we know them. (pp. 109-110)*

Similarly, Yogananda (1946) writes, "The pranic lifetrons in the spermatazoa and ova . . . guide the development of the embryo according to a karmic design" (p. 478n).

At any rate, for many people the amount of personal pain they carry would certainly seem restrictive, if not downright prohibitive, of the spiritual path. In these cases meditation can become long and arduous. The effect of a lot of second-line, repressed pain can be that one's meditation is continually plagued by disturbing thoughts and feelings rooted in various unconscious trauma.

An example of this sort of thing is given by Amodeo (1981). The method used to overcome this block is one that is a crucial feature of primal therapy.

# Meditation Can Bring Up Unresolved Traumas from Early Life

## One Can Hardly Remain Calm

In meditation it is true that one can open up to such completely forgotten experiences. Thus confronted, one could hardly remain calm and unaffected. In this way meditation can be disruptive and might even lead one into therapy. It is becoming increasingly known that this is not an uncommon result of meditation (cf. Epstein & Leiff, 1981; Walsh, 1979, p. 164). Consequently, some people enter primal therapy this way.

## Defusing Mental Contortions … Aiding Meditation

For these people it seems that primal is helpful in allowing them to relive these repressed experiences, thereby revealing connections to their troublesome conscious derivatives. This defuses such mental contortions and allows meditation to be practiced with less of these distractions. Or, in terms of the mechanics of meditation as described by Rama et al. (1976, pp. 149-151), the disturbing thoughts are allowed to invade consciousness totally and have complete sway. But as in doing so they reveal their origins, they are sent back to the unconscious, "elaborated" and "weighted" though they may be, but bound to their historical roots. Thus, when they arise again, either spontaneously in meditation or triggered outside meditation, they do not produce further elaborations — as in worrying, trying to figure them out, or self-abasement. And, if all elements of the complex have been uncovered, they can be much more easily dismissed by consciousness. The effect is that of aiding meditation in its attempt at dissipating thoughts, which are now mere tracings rather than stopped-up cauldrons.

## Otherwise, Meditation Can Become a Defense and Keep One Stuck in Struggling

It would seem that without a primal-type therapy, meditation could allow some gains in terms of glimpses of reality outside of one's inner dialogue, and some in terms of helping to dissipate the causes of that dialogue. Yet as long as there are experiences that are completely cut off from consciousness, and that, continually charged as they are, produce troublesome and distracting thoughts that feed the inner dialogue and must forever be dissipated, then meditation would not seem to be as effective in eliciting the gains that are possible. Under these circumstances meditation can become a defense and a struggle and serve to prohibit further growth (cf. Amodeo, 1981, p. 152; Epstein & Leiff, 1981, p. 145).

# 15

# Clean and Unclean Mysticism: The "Monsters" and Demons and Fear Do Not Exist Outside of You

*"You Haven't Lost Your Human Form Yet": Behind
Personal Fear and Pain We Discover a More Pervasive
Beauty and Bliss ... a Universe of Grace and Love.*

## Unclean Mysticism (Cerebral Distortion)

For many people the result of spirituality without primaling or some other cathartic technique is the existence of symbolized pain, the many "demons" within that must constantly be fought, resisted, and pushed out of the way in order to get glimpses of the underlying bliss, beauty, and love.

It is thus interesting to note the amount of evil, fear, and ugliness that is encountered in certain disciplines, especially primitive ones.

## "Allies"? Or, "Monsters"?

Carlos Castaneda's works contain much of this, and at one point he indicates why this is so in a manner that is parallel to the point being made here. He had just had an encounter with the "allies," which he had seen as grotesque monsters. In describing this to his companion, la Gorda, he begins to realize that she, who had been there also, had not seen the same things as he:

*"The allies have no form," she said when I had finished. "They are like a presence, like a wind, like a glow. The first one we found tonight was a blackness that wanted to get inside my body. . . . The others were just colors. Their glow was so strong, though, that it made the trail look as if it were daytime."*

## "You Haven't Lost Your Human Form Yet."

And further on:

*"Why do I see them as monsters?" I asked.*

*"That's no mystery," she said. "You haven't lost your human form yet. The same thing happened to me. I used to see the allies as people; all of them were Indian men with horrible faces and mean looks. They used to wait for me in deserted places. I thought they were after me as a woman. The Nagual used to laugh his head off at my fears. But still I was half dead with fright. One of them used to come and sit on my bed and shake it until I would wake up. The fright that ally used to give me was something that I don't want repeated, even now that I'm changed. Tonight I think that I was as afraid of the allies as I used to be."*

*"You mean that you don't see them as human beings anymore?"*

*"No. Not anymore. The Nagual told you that an ally is formless. He is right. An ally is only a presence, a helper that is nothing and yet is as real as you and me." (1977, pp. 151-152)*

## "Human Form" = Ego, Unreal Self, the Pain and Culturally Determined Cerebral Distortions

The "human form" referred to here is identical to what I have been calling the familiar cerebral pathways; one might also say "persona," ego, or "unreal self." It is the pain and culturally determined cerebral overlay through which we perceive reality. Presumably a person with less pain, or with access to a primal-type therapy, would have fewer "monsters" getting in the way of clear perception. Or, in Rowan's (1983, p. 24) words, "For the first time we can have a clean mysticism, not cluttered up with womb stuff, birth stuff, oral stuff, anal stuff, oedipal stuff, shadow stuff, anima stuff."

Thus, it is not that the existence of pain prevents larger perceptions; rather, it distorts them and makes them less accessible.

## "Human Form" — Cerebral Distortion — Makes for a "Polytheism" of Spiritual Understanding

It appears that some spiritual disciplines allow one to open up to parts of the mind that are preneurotic, but that in order to do so they often must cut through an incredible maze of symbolized pain and cultural overlay. Considering the myriad forms that this kind of distortion makes possible, one can speculate that it has much to do with accounting for the extent and variety of the spiritual phenomena that we see exhibited in the spiritual literature. Such distortions also can be viewed as contributing strongly to the diversity of religious concept, ritual, and artifact. Although the underlying reality may be the same for all of us and account for the similarities in concept and phenomena (as emphasized by Jung and others), the cerebral overlay can be seen to account for the vastly different contents of such.

# Clean Mysticism

## The "Monsters" Are not Real, A Pronoic Perspective ... An Essentially Benign Universe Characterized by Grace and Love

The contribution of a primal perspective, then, is twofold. First, it becomes obvious that the "demons," the "monsters," the resulting fear are not "real" (in terms of being rooted in transpersonal or "objective" reality). Rather, they are personal elements invading the perception of transpersonal reality. Behind the personal fear and pain we discover a more pervasive beauty and bliss, we sense an essentially benign universe characterized by grace and love.

## Exotic Phenomena ~ Spiritual Cotton Candy

Second, the primal perspective allows us to see that much of the exotic phenomena as described in the spiritual literature is a consequence of personal pain and predilection and is not real in the transpersonal sense.

# 16

# Deeper, and Higher, Spiritual Realities: Science Has Uncovered Something Subtler Than the Physical, Undergirding One's Life, and Interconnected with All and Everyone

*Essence of Archetype, Desymbolizing the World, and*
*Removing the Mask of Mysticism: The "God Above God"*

## Desymbolizing the World

### Making Exotic Phenomena Superfluous

These two conclusions — the "demons" not being real and spirituality's "exotic phenomena" being a product of personal pain — are sustained by the evidence that primalers are finding access to "cosmic life force" and "bliss" feelings often described in the spiritual literature, without having to contend with the monsters and demons, nor with the extravaganza of other-worldly description, which are concomitant to the life-force descriptions in the spiritual literature. Although one may reach deeper levels through various techniques, the deeper perceptions often are interpreted in terms of the highly symbolizing cortex. Bliss or life-force feelings are felt as immensely stronger and bigger than one's self, in relation to a consciousness narrowed by personal pain and culture. And thus, they lend themselves readily to hyperbole and transpersonal descriptions.

## Demythologizing Reality

Primal therapy performs its desymbolizing function, making the exotic phenomena superfluous, by connecting the symbolic material pervading normal consciousness to real-life events. This dissipates the value of any such symbolic material as something in its own right. In primal this demythologizing process is apparent where many of the activities and fantasies of daily life are found to be "act outs," that is, symbolizations of past pain: One reaches for a cigarette as symbolic of an unsatisfied need to nurse; or one becomes a writer because one was never listened to; or one travels the globe as symbolic of a need to be free of a constricting home environment in childhood.

# Essence of Archetype

But it seems that some of the deeper and more sensational experiences also are symbolic of primal pain. Even some of the "archetypal" experiences appear to be derivative of still deeper material. For example, I have relived a postnatal experience that involved the cutting, scrubbing, and general abuse of my body (which was part of postnatal infant "care" in hospitals when I was born).

I can see where I could easily have imbued the experience with fantasy elements of an archetypal "Terrible Mother."

I did not choose to do so, because that would have meant turning what was obviously a personal reality into a fantasy and into something "transpersonal." Yet I can also see where someone without access to the personal memory part of the experience would be left with only the fantasy.

## Archetypal Universality ~ Biological Universality

The experiences evident in primal therapy strongly indicate that much of what has usually been termed "transpersonal" are, in fact, symbolically derived from personal life experiences in the "personal unconscious," and that their seeming universality is related to our biological universality, especially as it concerns our gestation and birth.

Grof's research also indicates that much of the exotic phenomena is symbolized preverbal pain. Concerning first-line or perinatal phenomena under LSD, he notes

*The encounter with death on the perinatal level takes the form of a profound firsthand experience of the terminal agony that is rather complex and has emotional, philosophical, and spiritual as well as distinctly physiological facets. (1976, p. 96)*

## Prenatal and Perinatal Roots of Spirituality

But then he also points out:

*In a way that is not quite clear at the present stage of research, the above experiences seem to be related to the circumstances of the biological birth. LSD subjects frequently refer to them quite explicitly as reliving of their own birth trauma. Those who do not make this link and conceptualize their encounter with death and the death-rebirth experience in a purely philosophical and spiritual framework quite regularly show the cluster of physical symptoms described earlier that can best be interpreted as a derivative of the biological birth. They also assume postures and move in complex sequences that bear a striking similarity to those of a child during various stages of delivery. In addition, these subjects frequently report visions of or identification with embryos, fetuses, and newborn children. Equally common are various authentic neonatal feelings as well as behavior, and visions of female genitals and breasts. (p. 96)*

I am reminded of Muktananda describing one of his spiritual experiences in which he visits "hell" (1974, pp. 114-115), which is a world filled with excrement. His description has striking parallels to some LSD experiences noted by Grof (1976), wherein this is said to be associated with "the contact with such biological materials and the termination of the agonizing experience of birth" (pp. 130-131).

## Biological Basis of Myth

The fact that primalers relive these intrauterine and birth experiences without all of the accompanying symbolism, as exhibited in both the psychedelic and spiritual literatures, is evidence of a desymbolized cortex, less obscure in its perceptions. In fact, there is a pattern seen in the LSD research as well as, to a limited extent, in primal therapy: Upon subsequent relivings of a traumatic experience, such as one's birth, there is a tendency for initial, highly symbolized encounters with the material to be followed by sessions containing less symbolism. Typically, this occurs until the event finally is able to be accepted and relived in its real-life historical detail and, often, biological brutality (cf. Grof, 1976, pp. 68-69, 56, 58-60; 1977, p. 12).

# The "God Above God"

But although the experiences of primalers and LSD subjects serve to dispel much of what is thought of as transpersonal phenomena, there still is much that cannot be explained away as derivative of primal pain. I am not sure that I agree with Grof in the extent to which he attributes transpersonal status to certain elements that are intermingled with perinatal phenomena. He writes, for example: "Perinatal experiences represent a very important intersection between individual psychology and transpersonal psychology" (1976, p. 99).

## Deeper, and Higher, Spiritual Realities

But even without the pain-tainted elements, many of which have been called archetypal, it becomes increasingly hard to disregard his evidence for transpersonal phenomena on what appears to be a deeper level of the unconscious than even the perinatal. Certainly the prenatal arena has transpersonal overtones. Sperm and egg experiences themselves, in that they transcend the normal space/time boundaries of the personal in implicating a mechanism of memory that is nonphysical, are categorized by Grof as transpersonal experiences. Furthermore, beyond even that, the evidence from LSD research and the current spiritual literature suggests that the transpersonal level may be more expansive and varied than even Jung had envisioned.

Janov might dismiss these transpersonal experiences as "overload" phenomena, that is, as fantasies occurring out of released, painful energy that is too great to be dealt with. But because they occur when the perinatal phenomena have been thoroughly, not incompletely, worked through, and because they have such far-reaching and positive effects on personality and later behavior, I do not think they can be so easily discarded.

## Proof of "God"

Some of these experiences, especially in the parapsychological realm (such as ESP, clairvoyance, and ancestral memories), have even found verification with an astonishing degree of accuracy in Grof's follow-up research (1976, pp. 164-167, cf. p. 207). Even the primal perspective, which points to the existence of memory and consciousness at the fetal, single cell, and sperm and egg level, certainly would have to acknowledge such awareness to have more subtle underpinnings than the brain and spinal cord.

All of this points to the existence of something that is subtler than the physical body and undergirds the entire length of one's physical life. The evidence also seems to suggest that this subtler self permeates much of matter and life in realms outside of the personal domain and therefore can be accurately termed transpersonal.

# 17

## Zorba the Buddha: Enlightenment as an Attitude of Adventuring ... Eventually It Is Simply About Staying Open to Experience/Process

*Ecstasy Is Intensity ... Catharsis and Calmness in Spirituality: Spock Should Hardly Have Been the Poster Child for Mysticism ... What's so "Alive" About Acting Like a Machine?*

## The Big Primal ~ Instant Satori

Another perspective on this subject is suggested by Heider (1974). He says that an emphasis on catharsis is rooted in "a model of growth and transcendence based on the concept of the sudden satori" (p. 41), which is considered unrealistic. It is true that this situation existed among many primalers. Many of us initially, and in line with Janov's assertions, did assume this dependence on and/or expectation of the "big primal": the primal that would make it all different and change our lives forever. In fact, letting go of this expectation began to be seen as a mark distinguishing advanced from beginning primalers. More experienced primalers began to see primal as a tool, not an end in itself. We began to see ourselves as growing and living both inside and outside of our primaling, and to see feelings as going on all the time, not just when we were lying down and "catharting."

*...if we do not "be" with our illusions, we cannot know them...*

The initial confusion, however, is understandable, considering the inaccurate impression engendered by the early primal that all feeling that is not primaling is somehow unreal. This myth serves to negate all that passes through one and all that one feels between primal experiences. Janov was trying to make a point, and an important one at that: Much of what goes on inside one's self is, in fact, elements of primal complexes and therefore is not accurate perceptions of self, others, and world. But an important facet to this is that it remains important to "be" with all that material, whether objectively valid or not, in order that one may link it all together and have the connections and insights that can occur during those catalyzing events called primals. For if we do not "be" with our illusions, we cannot know them. Hence, how can we discard them?

Certainly the awesomeness of some forms of catharsis, the energy release involved, helps one to downplay the significance of the in-between times. But subsequently such plateau or calm spots, preparation or postcathartic periods, even the activities of our daily life, took on an importance previously unacknowledged. We began to understand that it is not a matter of catharsis for catharsis's sake, or just of emptying one's "Primal Pool," in Janov's terms.

In that sense I am in agreement with Heider's (1974, p. 41) direction in leaving an emphasis on catharsis and beginning "to rely heavily upon spiritual disciplines, both as preparation for the release of tension and as a maintenance program designed to enhance and prolong the desirable effects of the encounter experience." For, using meditation in the sense that Rajneesh (1976) does, that of being with where one is in the here and now, it makes perfect sense to me that a spiritual regimen can and should be used during the in-between times to help us to stop and be aware of the continuing process within us, if that is what it takes.

## Being Where One Is

An important sidelight, however, is that for many primalers this sort of structuring may be unnecessary. As mentioned, the results of primaling, in the postcathartic period, may be the same as the results of meditation. Consequently, for many advanced primalers access is only too apparent during the between times. Therefore, to "be" where one is often only requires that we leave off avoiding — through distracting ourselves in work, sex, alcohol, drugs, food, and various other ways — the primal/spiritual process that continues within us between sessions. At this point it becomes a matter of staying open to Experience/Process, allowing it to flow through and teach us.

## Meditation Can Be Anti-Spiritual

In fact, there is the known danger in using a spiritual technique that it can be used to defend against "process." As Epstein and Leiff (1981, p. 145) put it, "Meditation experiences may be used in both adaptive and defensive ways." And a meditation that is used solely to force us into relaxation or into a concentration with a specific focus as a way to defend against "process" and the occasional peaks and valleys that are part of it would, in my opinion, be antiprimal, indeed would be antispiritual, antimystical, antigrowth.

# Zorba the Buddha

Therefore, in general I agree with Heider's shift in emphasis away from catharsis and to the postcathartic period, but not nearly to the extent to which he apparently has. For I do not see a need to "transcend" catharsis or go "beyond" it as he does. Certainly Grof, Muktananda, and others would concur that even the outer reaches of transpersonal experience do not entail a cessation of conflict, resolution, growing, and learning. Similarly, Epstein and Leiff (1981, p. 144) have pointed out that "meditation can be viewed as a developmental process which can produce side effects anywhere along the continuum," and so one would wonder why we would leave off catharsis as a tool for dealing with such blocks.

## Ecstasy Is Intensity ... What Is so Alive About Being Machine-Like?

I should point out that the experience of nearly all primalers is that the need to cathart becomes less as time goes on. But additionally, I do not see a need to posit a point beyond catharsis, for I do not see anything wrong with catharsis, with enjoying the capacity to experience intensity of ecstasy, desolation, or insight. It seems to me that this capacity can add color and vitality to our lives. Indeed, it may be that which, at times, makes us feel we are alive!

## It Wouldn't Be "Up" if You Never Came "Down" from It

But Heider certainly does find something wrong with catharsis, and our differences bring up an important point. He points out that he left off inducing catharsis because of post-cathartic depression that would ensue. it is my opinion that occasional catharsis can have just that sort of effect if we acknowledge the depths of primal and perinatal phenomena extending all the way back through birth and womb material. Therefore, anything short of a thorough working through of these deeper levels always will leave one susceptible to relapses, postcathartic depressions, and return of symptoms in that these catharses represent further access as well as resolution.

## Enlightenment as an Attitude of Adventuring

To that extent, I believe that Heider has not gone far enough with catharsis to those areas where the most substantial gains can be made ... although even then we can expect "relapses" if we employ the model that Grof, among others, presents of "enlightenment" being an attitude toward the process of becoming, of adventuring deeper into the cosmos, rather than a static serene state of inaction. Grof has shown us how deep one often must go before one can expect real resolution; or, in other words, just how deep within us, and how far into our past, the roots of our present concerns extend.

## Spock is Hardly a Role Model for Spirituality

A passage from the *I Ching* may help to clarify this point. It is possible that because of our Appolonian Western heritage we have a tendency to view an unaffected, somehow undisturbable state … as in our common conceptions of the results of meditation … as a goal. But not all cultures and spiritual disciplines posit it as such. In the Wilhelm/Baynes classic translation of the ancient work it is written,

*While Buddhism strives for rest through an ebbing away of all movement in nirvana, the Book of Changes holds that rest is merely a state of polarity that always posits movement as its complement"* (p. 201).

Apparently, an unmovable state is seen as neither desirable nor possible; it is indicative of death rather than greater life.

It continues further on:

*True quiet means keeping still when the time has come to keep still, and going forward when the time has come to go forward.*

*In this way rest and movement are in agreement with the demands of the time, and thus there is light in life.*

*When a man has thus become calm, he may turn to the outside world. He no longer sees in it the struggle and tumult of individual beings, and therefore he has that true peace of mind which is needed for understanding the great laws of the universe and for acting in harmony*

*with them.*

*Whoever acts from these deep levels makes no mistakes.*

Such it is that we can be in the midst of life, fully experiencing it, and yet be aware of its illusionary quality, hence be unattached to it and more able to flow with it. Let us say, "Zorba the Buddha."[4]

# 18

# The Agonies and Ecstasies of Exquisiteness: The Psyche Heals Itself … If Only Allowed to Do So

*"The Only Way Out Is All the Way In": The Eye of the Hurricane, The Cosmic Adventure, and Being Here … Why Would Reality Not Be Real?*

## The Eye of the Hurricane

From this view we see that it is our attitude toward intense experiences, not whether or not we have them, that is important. The I Ching addresses this in the hexagram, "The Arousing (Shock/Thunder)": "The shock causes no loss, because one takes care to stay in the center of the movement and in this way to be spared the fate of being tossed hither and thither" (p. 200).

## "The Only Way Out Is All the Way In"

One is reminded of Heider's statement that new members of a group may be badly frightened in viewing another member who, in the midst of catharsis, feels no feelings of fear about it (1974, p. 37). Or, as one primaler put it, "It is not feeling one's feelings that is really painful" (cf. Janov, 1970, pp. 98-99). Thus, by plunging in and surrendering to it, one can be aware of a calm center within the chaos that is imperceptible on the periphery. Or, in another primaler's words, "The only way out is all the way in."

## Again, Be the Observer

Thus, it is a matter of whether or not we get caught up in intense experiences and make them part of a personal drama ... "acting out" is the primal way of saying it ... or we simply allow them to flow through us. In the first case, we give these feelings a status in our lives they do not deserve and increase the time required to work through them; in the second, we maintain an attitude as of a channel for experience, not an originator of it.

## Cosmic Adventure

In this regard, we note Grof's statement that at advanced levels of transpersonal experience, beyond ego death and rebirth, "it becomes . . . a cosmic adventure in consciousness aimed at solving the riddles of personal identity, human existence, and the universal scheme" (1980, p. 215). Or in other words, we still carry water, but we are not attached to it.

# Process Is Process

Therefore, I am saying that much has been made of a difference between primal and meditation for what is primarily a difference in technique. Both can be seen as ways of attuning us to a spiritual/growth process that is common to us all, affecting our daily happenings and the life choices and directions we take in either direct or distorted fashion.

## Meditation Is Technique. It Is not the Process Itself

For meditation the confusion seems to have arisen from viewing it as the sole means to growth, rather than simply a means to get in touch with a process that is growthful both inside and outside of meditation. And when we open up, what arises always is different from what we expect and includes all sorts of phenomena and experiences, all linked to our growth and resolving our blocks.

## Primal Aids Learning Surrender

Likewise, an important benefit of primal is that it can teach us an attitude of surrender to process. That we can throw ourselves, time and again, into the maelstrom of catharsis and still, somehow, be upheld and even embraced, despite ourselves, gives us confidence in a beneficent universe and allows us to foster surrender in our attitudes to the pushes and pulls of process as it makes itself known to us in our daily life.

## Being Here

Both meditation and primal can be seen as techniques to help us "be" where we are "at." And to be most fully where we are means to be most fully in process. So it is just that at times they employ different means to get us in touch with the underlying flow that is the epigenetic protagonist of healing and creation, growth and transcendence.

And once attuned to process, one can "be here" while working, walking, primaling, or engaging in "zazen"; it then becomes ludicrous to talk of different techniques or different levels of growth. Ultimately, when we are "on track" the process takes over, leading us onward to more encompassing realms, regardless of how we get on track.

Evidence for this is given by meditation research as cited by Earle (1981). Although physiological correlates differ with different techniques at beginning levels, later stages show a convergence of the correlates.

# The Psyche Heals Itself

## ... If Allowed to Do So

There are striking similarities in the descriptions of the deep-level growthful experiences found in the spiritual literature, the psychedelic literature, the ethnographic literature, and in some of our primal reports. But what we find, in primal anyway, is that the psyche "heals" itself, if only allowed to do so, and in a way that is reminiscent of the way the body does. And so it is not so surprising that the manner in which it does so would be so similar in different places, at different times, and using different techniques for allowing it.

## Why Would Reality Not Be Real?

It is equally not surprising that we should find examples of spiritual phenomena occurring during primaling or "primal" phenomena occurring during meditation, or either occurring under LSD. For why would we expect to have anything but a common heritage and for reality to be other than itself? Is it not only our dichotomizing mind that construes such dualities to obscure and make more difficult the path that we commonly tread, that tragically serves to neutralize the compassion and interrelatedness that we would otherwise feel?

## The Agonies and Ecstasies of Exquisiteness

The point being made is that the primal process of which we speak is the same as the spiritual process. Both catharsis and calmness are natural parts of the same flow, mingling and alternating with each other, and emanating from each other, sometimes in a linear way. This flow is a natural process of creation that encompasses both types of phenomena, the agonies and ecstasies of existence, and harmonizes all of reality, both internal and external, in a pattern that is unique for every individual and oriented toward one's patient unfolding in the path of exquisiteness.

# Summary of "A Primal Perspective on Spirituality"

Contrary to Janov's assertion that spiritual experience is derivative of primal pain, there is evidence that primalers are encountering transpersonal phenomena at a deeper level of the primal process. I relied on my experiences and those of other long-term primalers, along with the evidence of meditation and LSD research and the current spiritual literature, in proposing an alternative explanation of the relationship between catharsis and spiritual process in which they are seen as complementary, not opposed, processes.

At a certain level of the spiritual process "primal-type" experiences often occur, no matter how interpreted. A primal-type therapy, therefore, can be an invaluable, perhaps indispensable, aid in higher consciousness. Primal therapy reduces the symbolic clutter and cerebral "noise" that characteristically obscure the perception of spiritual realities. It thereby enables spiritual access that would be unavailable to some people conceived into less than ideal life situations. Beyond the primal-type levels of the spiritual process, deeper levels are encountered that do not give indications of containing elements of repressed pain or need, and that can be accurately termed transpersonal.

Therefore, primal therapy and meditation represent an identity of ends and an antithesis of means. Both catharsis and meditation are techniques to help us to "be" where we are "at" and thereby to be more fully in a "process" that transcends techniques. For "when we are 'on track,' the process takes over, leading us onward to more encompassing realms, regardless of how we get 'on track.'"

# SECTION THREE

# A FORAY INTO CELLULAR-TRANSPERSONAL CONSCIOUSNESS

# 19

## The Spirituality of Cells and Seeds of Light in Every Darkness: All the Things We Do in Life Are Distant Reflections of Our Earliest Life as Cells

*The Experience of Simultaneous Fractals That Is Life ...*
*The Toilsome Life of Cells: It Ain't Easy Being Sperm*

## Cellular/Transpersonal Experiences

Having established the legitimacy of transpersonal aspects of prenatal, and especially cellular, re-experience, it remains to be seen what light this new perspective throws upon traditional formulations. I suggest to you that this perspective is a catalyst to a radical reformulation of traditional concepts of consciousness and development. My understanding is that it supports a view compatible with Eastern, Platonic, and "primitive" philosophical renderings — which can be characterized as *Emanationist* — and completely undermines the dominant Western evolutionary paradigm. I delineate such a perspective, which I call the Falls from Grace Theory, beginning in the next section, Section Four.

However, let us first take a look at a sampling of the kinds of experiences and perspectives that are possible at this cellular and prenatal level of re-experience before attempting to see deeper into the structure of consciousness and development, presented immediately afterwards, which contains and makes sense of them. The current section — "A Foray Into Cellular-Transpersonal Consciousness" — contains transcripts of cellular/transpersonal experiences I had through the modality of holotropic breathwork. In order to retain the flavor and potency of the raw experience itself, these transcripts are only slightly edited and are from the descriptions of my experiences I recorded immediately after having them.

# Just a Membrane Away (February 8, 1992)

## Physicality Just Feels Sickening

An important thing that happened during the holotropic session was that after experiencing sperm feelings, and going into the egg, and the egg swirling around … in the beginning there was a lot of heavy duty nausea, a lot of it. I was very sick. I felt like I remember being sick like that at certain times of my life, and I just wanted to die. And I felt like I was back there at the beginning of life and feeling how shitty it is to be physical, right from the beginning … and feeling like: yes, this is what characterizes the physical plane; physicality just feels sickening.

And then there was a bhajan tape on. And I couldn't help thinking lots of times about my Sai Baba connection and even picturing Puttaparthi and everything. There were several different bhajans. And suddenly I got this whiff of incense out of nowhere [there was no incense anywhere in the room]. And then I made the connection that I was feeling exactly the way I was feeling in Puttaparthi when I had dysentery. And it came to me that I had not fully processed the pain I'd gone through over there. And so here it was coming up again prompted by the smell of incense.

## Nausea Goes All the Way Back to the Beginning ... Everything That Happens, Even Sickness, Is Part of Spiritual Process

And I was making the connection, thinking about how I haven't wanted to burn incense since that time because it's associated with that feeling of nausea. And since that nausea goes all the way back to the beginnings, when we first came into life, it makes sense that I wouldn't want to be triggered into that. I also realized that Baba had been setting me up to feel these feelings, about sperm and egg and everything, through the getting of the dysentery and how He was taking me to some pretty profound feelings over there — just in getting sick and dealing with life being a life and death matter and wanting to leave it and deciding to stay and everything.

## Primordial Evil and Its Relation to Pain

Other things that happened: I got a glimpse into some primordial evil. At one point I started to feel real powerful, and there were a series of images of war in my consciousness. And I could understand how people could murder and rape, because it was so powerful to be caught up in stuff like that rather than to feel the pain of the body. And it dawned on me that I could easily have been murdering and raping in other lifetimes and that other people do also.

## Even Warring Feels Better Than Feeling One's Emotional Pain

And it's got to do with how we come into this life and there's all this pain in the physical body, and we act it out in all kinds of ways, including getting caught up in wars and things which are just this hyped-up organized energy which seems better than feeling the pain. And that was a pretty grisly area to look at about physicality and the horror that exists in it.

# It Ain't Easy Being Sperm

I also realized that I was feeling tremendously exhausted going through the sperm ... egg ... and I was having some blastocyst feelings for the first time. I was feeling like I was multiplying. At one point I felt as though I were trying to connect with the uterine wall and all kinds of things like that. There were, occasionally, good feelings, but mostly it was pretty uncomfortable and not nice.

## Understanding The Core of Pain ... "Life Is a Prison."

One thing that occurred to me: Of course I want to transcend the physical plane! I said when I introduced myself in the go-around before the workshop that I'd done this hundreds of times in the last twenty years; and I've been born literally into hundreds of lives, and I'm tired of coming here, and feeling this pain. And it occurred to me that that is what Baba is doing to me — having me get right to the core of understanding pain, so I can decide finally to give up this addiction to the physical plane and stop coming back here. At one point, for example, at the end, it occurred to me, as Baba had said: "It's a prison."

## The Experience of Simultaneous Fractals That Is Life ... The Toilsome Life of Cells

After the sperm and egg feelings, and the egg getting nauseated going down the fallopian tube, and the conception feelings, I was having these feelings that were like cells multiplying. I was also feeling like a zygote and my hands were going out, taking things in and throwing things out. I was thinking how everything in my life is a reenactment of these early things, like right down to the tiniest things like taking tissues in and throwing phlegm out while I'm lying here in this workshop.

## Seeds of Light in Every Darkness

I remember one spot in the experience where I was feeling the imperfection on the physical plane, and then at one point in that Mary Lynn [my wife and the person who was my "sitter," or attendant, during the experience] had water ready for me. And so I realized there are some good things here too, that there is love, and so on — some flashes of light in it all.

# 20

# We Are Always and Only "Just a Membrane Away" … from Understanding Everything: "Juicy Caring" and the Answer to Pain

*"I Couldn't Believe How Much Caring I Had Inside of Me":*
*Underneath It All the Only Juicy Thing That Makes Life*
*Worth Living Is this Feeling of Connection with Everybody*

## Cellular Beginnings of Desire: Sperm and Egg … Reflections of Universal Love/Attraction

I did have a lot of opening and closing of my legs also. I even had some egg-welcoming-the-sperm feelings at the same time as I was feeling like I wanted something; I wanted to reach out and hug the music it was so beautiful.

And the movements of my hands made me realize I was like the egg pulling in the sperm. I had an insight into how the egg wanted to unite with the sperm and what it's like to want to unite with something — to have something wonderful on this physical plane with all this pain … that there are some things that you want, and that's why the egg pulls the sperm in.

## Being One Cell … You One-Celled Animal You!

Again there was a lot of lying there and feeling like a one-celled animal, and that being both good and bad and if nothing else, being different. At one point I remember focusing on all these feelings and they weren't good and they weren't bad, just different. They were interesting.

## The Immensity of Experience

I kept on thinking about the immensity of experience. The music kept having me look into all these areas of experience from all these times and places and everything else — physical and non-physical, never been physical, and so on. All this universe of experience … and I just kept tapping into it, all these spaces. And a lot of it wasn't great or bad; it was just different. I can't say I really liked it; but if you're going to be here, it's interesting to see what all there is.

And I went through a period where I wasn't quite feeling conscious; and all kinds of things were happening that were almost on a dream level, that had to do with shapes and forms.

# Juicy Caring

Finally, towards the end, music came up that made me really cry. And it had to do with feeling or thinking about all the people in my life and all their pain … and my pain, but mostly theirs, and all the people that are sad. I had a strong sense of connection and caring for them. I couldn't believe how much caring I had inside of me. It was a real juicy feeling. I felt like I was feeling something fundamental, like when I was a kid.

## Connection With All and Everyone

I kept thinking about how when we are in our *hylotropic* mode [that is to say, the everyday consciousness mode], we go away from these kinds of things, from those kinds of feelings. We get caught up in things and plans and duties, but underneath it all the only juicy thing that makes life worth living is this feeling of connection with everybody. I kept thinking as an example how Mary Lynn and I, when we watch TV and see all the pain of people around the world, and how we really feel a connection with these people and we cry for them and their pain.

## Why We Turn from Caring

And that's how it felt, that's how it felt when I was a kid before I had to shut down because the pain was overwhelming. It's just too overwhelming to see people like my father and my mother, my older brother, all these people in my life who have so much pain.

## "I Really Want to Help" — The Answer to Pain

I felt like I was actually primaling for them, for the world; letting out the feelings of pain for the whole world, and I felt like I really wanted to do that; I really wanted to help. I realized how that is my major motivation: I really want to help.

I realized that is the answer to pain, that's why I'm doing all the reading, looking so hard in all those books I'm reading. There's no end to the amount of books I want to read, because right around the corner I may find the answer to pain. And I'll be doing it for myself but mostly for the whole world. I want to help the pain stop.

# Just a Membrane Away … from Satori

And then at another part of it, it was almost like there was a membrane around me. And I could sense there was something wonderful which was like the spiritual reality, that we were just a membrane away from it; we're always just a membrane away from it.

And especially me, my whole life I've felt like I've been on the edge of this spiritual reality and caught on the physical plane, caught in my own consciousness and just a fuckin' short jitterbug away was this wonderful bright yellow existence, this whole wonderful perspective about everything.

## Feeling "Juicy"

Actually it's this juicy feeling about everything, and what makes life meaningful is the occasional upsurge of this juicy feeling that just gives you a feeling of something that makes it all worthwhile — some reason to be here.

And I feel like that is probably the reality on the spiritual plane all the time, and that we just get glimpses of it here; and I feel like it's just a membrane away. And my whole life I've been just a membrane away from it, and just striving to find the answer to getting there, to find the answer to what this is all about.

# 21

# Life Is a Sickness … for the Purpose of Getting Us Well: There Is Always Grace

*Love Is "Just a Membrane" Away: No Matter How Bad It*
*Gets, There Is Always Something to Keep You Here … to*
*Comfort You When You Really Need It*

## The Real Reasons for Being Alive

Another thing I was thinking about in the course of my session was what good work this holotropic breathwork is and how — regardless of what I had been thinking about it when I was doing it with Stan Grof a couple of weeks ago — that I feel like this is certainly taking me to *all kinds* of goddamn places. It's certainly getting me past where I was in primal, getting me beyond that; so certainly it's damn good stuff.

I mean I just kept thinking that this is something that reminds people of the real reasons for being alive; and if that's not important, nothing is. But, if nothing else, I sure as hell felt: it works! The music was great; it did all kinds of wonderful things to me, taking my mind into all kinds of incredible places; it was almost like being stoned or like being on acid.

## Cosmic Frown

I remember thinking at one point about Mary Lynn and the cat and the dog that I had when I was a kid. I was thinking about how much pain there is in existence, and how my life has been in pain. For example, there was one time when my face just went into this incredible frown, and I was crying and crying after the frown happened. I began to realize how that was my essence: this Frown, a big part of me — there's just so much sadness in my life. I was thinking about what just happened recently with my father and all kinds of stuff. There was just so much sadness.

## But There Is Always Grace

I was grieving hugely for that, and then I was also thinking about how there were also things in my life that were good — like Mary Lynn and the cat. And I was thinking about our trailer, and about the kind of a life I have now, the cozy times we have. And then I was thinking about how there was that dog when I was younger, various cats, and so on. And I was thinking about that time in Puttaparthi when that cat came to me, and I realized how there had always been something — that no matter how much pain there was, there was never too much pain. That's when I got into the feelings about the membrane, or maybe that wasn't when I got into those feelings.

# Life Is a Sickness ... to Get Us Well

It was as if your needs are taken care of in some way or other. Life really was a sickness. But the sickness was for the purpose of you getting eventually healthy, that you weren't given more sickness than you could handle; there was always something to alleviate the pain, to enable you to continue on; that you would always be able to stay one step above the "pit" so to speak. You would be kept above it.

## The Fact That You Only Get as Much as You Can Handle Is Evidence of the Divine in Life

Your purpose here was not to be "tortured" or irrevocably damaged by pain — it was to be able to learn from pain, but mercifully so, so there was always something to keep you here and to comfort you when you really needed it. And I was feeling like that was God's evidence in our lives, that He's always just a membrane away, making sure it doesn't get too extreme here.

## Joyful Compassion

One last thing I should mention is that after this final crying during my breathing session — about all these people in my life and my connection with them and that juicy feeling I had when I was a kid caring for everybody, really wishing I could do something to help all my family, and not feeling that I was helpless, but really caring, really wanting to help — well there was this feeling of huge compassion, and it was a good feeling. I mean it was actually joyful — it's hard to describe.

## A Place on Which to Stand

But anyway after that I was left with this huge, very deep feeling of relaxation like I have rarely experienced, if ever. And I didn't want to come out of it. I lay there for a while after that feeling like I was an energy field, especially in my hands. I felt like a locked-in energy field just buzzing, and I didn't want to come back. I was so calm, not in pain, so comfortable that I felt like I wanted to keep this feeling with me always; it would be a wonderful place to come from in the world, to have inside me, to stand on, from which to view the world....

# 22

# Past Lives, Other Lives, and The Vast Hole of the "Not the Tribal": Sidling Up to the Implicate Order

*Warriors, Priests, Cells, and a Juicy Glowing Blastocyst on the Rise: Western Culture Has Created This Vast Hole in People ... Primal Desire ... and Love*

## A Juicy Glowing Blastocyst on the Rise (February 8, 1992)

I was just thinking how the mandala that I drew earlier was a picture of my feelings, but it ended up looking like I was this glowing blastocyst: And I was trying to reach out to these cells. And what that was representing was my juicy feeling, wanting to help all these people that I felt connected with, like my family. I realized how that's a feeling that's gone with me throughout my life, and so it's amazing how this reflects a certain biological stage in our early life.

What the mandala was showing was this juicy glowing blastocyst — which I felt I was when I was lying in that comfortable space coming up out of this underlying blue, comfortable, wonderfully comfortable, blue waves; with all these black signs of pain trying to fuck with it, and put out its light, but at the same time wanting to reach out to these other people [these other cells].

But it looks like the blastocyst is coming out from the spirit world, and it's being attacked by all these one-celled animals that want to eat it up or something — which could be something biological — but it wants to reach out to connect with the uterine wall. Incredible.

# A Ball of Experience, or Sidling Up to the Implicate Order (February 9, 1992)

## Past Lives, Other Lives

I want to add this to my holotropic experiences of yesterday. There were times when I felt like the music was tapping me into all kinds of experiences; it was all just a ball of experience, and the music was giving me glimpses of what experience was like in all kinds of different ways, all different parts of time and space; and it was fascinating.

It wasn't all either good or bad — it was just different, interesting. In fact a lot of it was not even good — it's just that it was so different it made it interesting.

## Warriors, Priests

I did have the sense at one point that maybe there was a couple of past lives that I was tapping into. And one concerned my being a priest. I remember my feelings of wanting to put my hands up in the motion of blessing somebody with the sign of the cross, and how that seemed so natural to me. In tapping into this I had the sense of myself dressed as a priest and having my hands like that — it felt natural.

Another past life concerned something which was entirely opposite. I don't remember what that was: perhaps a warrior. And then there have been feelings recently of identifying with black community and black lifestyle; feeling very wonderful and natural and "at home" in that way of being.

# The Implicate Order As Uterine Wall (February 9, 1992)

## And Cells

Another note: After I looked at my mandala, it occurred to me that the people I was trying to reach out to could be thought of as cells, which I as a blastocyst was trying to implant into. And in the course of the sharing that followed the holotropic session, I felt myself distinctly unresponded to, that I had reached out several times and got no response from all the people around me.

This seemed to reflect exactly what the situation would have been on the cellular level. It's possible this was indicating that I as a blastocyst was trying to implant into the cellular wall and found no response, found it to be difficult, and that the uterine wall was unresponsive.

This relates to how I perceive my mother to have probably been emotionally unresponsive to my needs and my desires to connect with her. This relates to my feelings of total despair when I'm unable to get through to Mary Lynn, and also to my feelings of despair and agony in not being able to get through to my family — who can now be seen as reflecting these various cells that I'm trying to connect with.

# The Vast Hole of the "Not the Tribal" (April 27, 1992)

The session today was pretty uneventful; I'm pretty tired.

There was one somewhat profound thing that happened though. And it had to do with a particular piece of music that sounded like African tribal men who were chanting real fast at one point. And then there was what sounded like an old woman doing this real squeaky-sounding thing with her voice, which was part of what they were supposed to be doing all together, and it was integrated with the rest. And all together it was a very bizarre sounding piece of music, with drums.

## Primal Desire ... and Love

And what it triggered in me was as follows: I had been having these feelings of just loving the music even though it was strange. I had been doing that for several pieces, even though it was strange; and I wanted more and more of it. In fact, I was reaching out to grab it [the music], like I was a blastocyst reaching out to connect with the wall or something, or like I was an egg reaching out to connect with the sperm. And it was that kind of great desire — just loving it.

## The Beauty of It All

I was thinking over and over again about the beauty, the beauty of it all, how beautiful everything is. And then I began to realize it was love, and then there was this feeling of being like in a primal setting [like being in a primal culture, tribe] and feeling what it's like to be loving everybody and wanting them, and thinking that they were beautiful ... so beautiful to be alive and to be with people.

And it was just this feeling of love for them and beauty about being alive.

## We Do Not Have a Tribe

And then I thought about myself being in this place [in the holotropic training group], and I thought it was similar. But there was also something different, which was that the Western world did not have tribes. People are brought up separate from each other, and the Western culture has created this vast hole in people and how that wasn't bearable, all the time we were in existence. And it's just the saddest thing, about this gigantic hole in each and every one of us because none of us had a home, we lacked that place where we belonged, we did not have a tribe.

Another strange aspect of this session was whereas I really enjoyed the music, and the music could not be loud enough for me in the beginning, afterwards it seemed too loud. I didn't like it at all then.

# 23

# The Sound of Creation and Cellular Template of Eternal Bliss: I Was This Pulsating One-Celled Animal … Each Reaching Out Was Joy of Being Alive

*"Bliss to Exist": A Strong Plant Blossoming, Digging Deep and Casting High, 'Tis Bliss to Exist.*

## The Sound of Creation, or "'Tis Bliss to Exist" (April 28, 1992)

It's the holotropic session of Tuesday of the first module. It started out with a long period of movement and that mid-space between consciousness and unconsciousness, and it was okay.

And then just like yesterday, it was right about in the middle that a certain musical piece started to be really delicious; and I couldn't help wanting to breathe with it and become part of it more and just express my feeling of deliciousness. And I started to breathe more and started to enjoy breathing more with the music and moving a little with the music, and then at a certain point the sperm movement started to happen in my body.

And then it was shortly after that when I recognized certain egg feelings in me. Again I was feeling this deliciousness, a feeling of attraction and desiring, just loving everything, loving the music, and my hands were going out to the sides. I was going into all kinds of opening and closing movements, almost like a sea creature or sea vegetable. My hands were going all kinds of ways, like a floating movement; but then I became centered on these egg movements, like bringing in, and my body came together this one time very much like what Graham Farrant talks about when he describes bringing your arms together and bringing the egg in; and so there was that kind of a thing going on.

And after a while I was lying there and I felt rather round; I was feeling amazingly round. And I remember the last thing — when I was feeling like I was the egg — my hands went out to the sides and I was waving them up and down. And it was this amazing feeling of softness in my hands. It was like I was in an altered state, hard to describe.

But I began to feel like I was switching into a different mode of consciousness, like I was on a strange drug, or I was becoming a different kind of a creature.

But then after that there was this sensation of feeling very big, very round rather. And then it was just these small movements in my hands, and my hands reaching out and putting something back, reaching out and putting something back; and it was going on in my hands and my legs.

And that went on for a little while, and then it started to get more and more. A lot of it was the music, like wanting to take in the music. Or I was doing it in tune with the music, like I was this pulsating one-celled animal.

And then the most amazing part of it was that as this one-celled animal I was expanding, getting bigger. It was a wonderful feeling, and there was also a sense of power. It was a beautiful feeling; and then this piece of music came on with a sense of power to it.

I was reaching my hands and legs in four directions, like reaching out, reaching out my hands and my feet. And I realized that this was my bliss in life, this sense of reaching out and expanding, getting to know more and more, getting to be more and more, getting to be more and more creative in more directions. This is the bliss that I follow, and it's making me happier and happier in my life right now.

It was like, here I was, right from the beginning, feeling this bliss as an early template, as a fertilized egg becoming more and more, expanding and multiplying; it's that wonderful feeling of expanding and multiplying and reaching out more and more, just an infinite amount of more is out there to reach out to.

And it was just so much; I had this feeling like "God," or maybe I was God; this was a God-like feeling, but this was the bliss of God; this is what it is all about, this expanding and reaching out, eternal experience, eternal bliss.

It was just so wonderful that I had to start expressing it, I had to vocalize it, little by little, with sounds coming out of me, almost synchronistically, with the music. Like I didn't plan it that way but these sounds like "ooooooh" and "oooo" started coming out of me with the music. They were the only expression for that wonderful feeling I was having that I could think of. It was the only proper expression of that wonderful feeling, and I began to realize there was a real lack of ways to express the bliss, that there were many ways to express pain, but so few ways to express joy and bliss. We are really limited in this way.

And physically it was like my hands were expressing this bliss; each time I reached out it was this wonderful feeling of joy and just being alive.

And I also began to realize a connection with the haiku I had written. The haiku was a perfect premonition of what I was now feeling — the haiku being,

A strong plant blossoming,

Digging deep and casting high,

'Tis bliss to exist.

That was a perfect premonition, because that's exactly what it felt like to me when I was stretching in each direction: digging deep and casting high, taking in and then throwing it out again as far as I could ... and this wonderful feeling of power and bliss in being able to do this and knowing that it was endless, eternal. It was bliss, and so I expressed that for a long time.

# 24

## The Bliss of Connection with Others … But There Is a Pain in Unexpressed Love: Womb with a Review

*A Review of Womb Life: I Was Experiencing Creation … and the Sensuous Wonderful Feeling of Being Alive and Growing….*

And then I seemed to tire of that, or the music changed. And after a while I went into a period where I felt like I didn't want to be on my back, and I went to one corner of the mat. And I told myself it was because it was wet where I'd been, but I went to one corner and I lay on my side.

And all of a sudden that made sense. My hands were moving like little fetal hands; and I was still feeling blissful. In fact I was thinking: "I don't want to become a big baby and have BPM II." I just wanted to stay a blastocyst. But I noticed that even as a fetus I was still grocking and digging and having a great time; and the music was still wonderful and I was still floating around. I still had movement in my hands and in my body to go with the music, to just groove with the rhythms of existence. And I felt like I was getting bigger. It seemed like I was going through a stage where I was really fetal, on my side. But then I felt the need to get up on my knees. And there was this really strong compulsion to get, like, on my head, to have my head down, and to have all the weight in my neck.

And when I did that finally — and it took me a while to get into that position, because it felt like the confines of gravity were working against me — I just wanted to tumble! But I couldn't do that because I wasn't in a gravityless situation. But eventually when I did get into that position it felt very right. And that was pretty good, too, but it was kind of cramped. And so I eventually stopped — it was too painful to maintain very long.

So I turned over on my side and just listened to the music. And then I spent a lot of time just listening to the music and realizing how great it was to exist and how beautiful it all is and how beautiful people are. And I began to think that that's why we come here, to have this wonderful experience of reaching out to people.

And I began to realize that the blastocyst knows somehow that it's reaching out to everyone else in the universe, even when it's just a blastocyst. It's reaching out because it knows the bliss of connecting with others. And the mandala that I envisioned would just be these cells multiplying outward with these snakelike arms reaching out in several directions to spin oneself around, or to reach out for more, or to just reflect the sensuous wonderful feeling of being alive and growing.

This is great. I'm really glad I'm doing this, and I hope I can continue to capture these feelings and to come from this space.

I want to say one other thing, and that's that I realized at one point that I used to do things where — when I'd have a holotropic or a primal session — that I would go and do a review of all my past issues of pain. It was almost like doing a summary first, and then at the end I might get into something new. But I would often do the summary: Like I would sometimes be repeating the trauma of not having my mother after birth — and my lips would be sucking and there'd be nobody there; and going through the pain of getting out of the womb — being stuck in the womb; and just do that whole repeat. And then sometimes after doing all of that I'd go into sperm feelings.

But this time it was as if my body was doing a review, a summary of all that I'd learned: life from sperm to egg, fertilized egg, blastocyst, all the way to fetus, and then all the way to the second stage, all the way to BPM II — like the whole sequence of BPM I was being reviewed. And I thought this is a much better time to be doing a review of than of what happens later on, after the pain starts [from BPM II onwards, as mentioned in the previous paragraph].

So this is what I was experiencing, this wonderful being a creative process. I was experiencing creation. They say Om is the sound of creation, the creative sound; everything comes from that — the primordial sound, primordial symbol. So I kept wondering if my "ohing" sounds would turn into Om [it never exactly did].

One other thing: I was feeling one time how what I was expressing was the feeling of love, that I was feeling love and expressing that. And that there is a pain in unexpressed love; the pain [of life] is that we express all our pain [and suffer through all that], and we don't get to feel the great love, which is kept in check.

And the pain is that the love is not able to be fully felt or released unless we do this kind of work, of course.

# 25

# Tribes and Wonder Versus Civilization and Suffering: More Nestling Up With the Implicate Order, Or Before and After the Western Fall (Split)

*The Priests in the Church Were Keeping Out All the Screaming People, Forcibly Repressing, Refusing to Acknowledge It*

## More Nestling Up With the Implicate, Or Before and After the Western Fall (Split) (June 19, 1992)

This is a holotropic session of this day:

It started out when the music was very rhythmic, and my hands were doing a lot of fertilized-egg kinds of movements and embryonic kind of stuff. And sometimes I was having images of Prague and of inside the city — especially Old Town Square and the towers. [Prague is where the holotropic workshop was being held.]

And I kept having pictures of people who had lived here, and all the suffering that had gone on here, and the striving. I kept picturing the people who had lived and written books and everything, plays and philosophies, inside their little rooms — all the different kinds of lives that people had here [Prague].

I kept picturing Swami [Sathya Sai Baba] and kept saying: "Oh Swami," as if I were feeling and acknowledging what had gone on here: the feelings and desires, the struggles and the yearnings, and all those human things and feelings that had passed through this place. And I felt sad for all these people, the hardship they had gone through and all the feelings. And then I got up and went to the bathroom.

And when I came back it was just very peaceful. The drumming and everything was just something that was there. And I enjoyed parts of it: There were African parts, and they would have drumming and I would understand what it would be like to be an African person in a tribe.

At one point, however, the African tribe music sounded different or not good. And I had the feeling that this was singing from another tribe, not my own, an enemy tribe or something; I didn't like it.

And then as it went off into different phases of music I would often feel very good — very interesting and beautiful in a certain way. And then it went into Native American chanting; and I thought that was incredible, that I must have been an indigenous American at one time ... just wonderfully beautiful.

And it was either just before or just after that there was this Gregorian-type Church music. And one of the things that I kept having — scenes from Prague going through my head the entire time — and one of the scenes was the inside of a church.

And when the Gregorian music came on, I pictured the inside of that church again. And one of the interesting things was I realized at a certain point that people in the room around me were screaming [they actually were, in reality] — and there was a lot of that going on — and I had this feeling as if — when the Gregorian music was on — that the people in the church, the priests that is, that they had this reality going on in which they were keeping out all the screaming people, they were keeping them all outside the church, trying to repress that, trying to deny the reality of that. And so I felt like I was tuning into the reality of this place: That they [the priests and ecclesiasts] would forcibly try to repress this other element and keep it out of their consciousness, would refuse to acknowledge, let alone deal with it.

# An Afterthought

As many as thirty million women were murdered horribly over a period of three hundred years during the middle ages for having any trace of free-mindedness. This was done under the direction of the Catholic Church. They were often burned at the stake.

It is no coincidence that what followed for the next four hundred years of Western "civilization" was a pall of Stepford wifery unparalleled among the cultures of humans, which we are only with great difficulty over the last hundred years awakening from.

Yet these forces of repression and murder continue with us today wishing to take us back to such middle age benighted views. They exist in the anti-abortion movement, even among mainstream Republicans, again with women as the direct target. And they exist in the Tea Party and conspiracy circles, even among some progressives, where feminism and progressive-liberal ideas are called "illuminati" — showing again that free-thinking women and enlightened views will not be tolerated ... and will be scapegoated for all the horrors of the top one percent and the powers that be, just as they were in the times of Catholic tyranny.

By the way, I have been misunderstood if anyone thinks this is just an attack on the Catholic Church. The Catholic Church was the primary evil *then*. I mentioned Western civilization. There are many more evil perpetrators today. It is not about blaming any institution. This is a product of our "civilization" and its anti-body, anti-sexual, anti-Nature insanity and the inherent evil of hierarchical societies in general.

PART 2


# FALLS FROM GRACE: A DEVOLUTIONAL MODEL OF CONSCIOUSNESS INCORPORATING PRE/PERINATAL PSYCHOLOGY AND SPECTRUM-TRANSPERSONAL PHILOSOPHY

# SECTION FOUR

# BIOLOGY AS METAPHOR
# AND MYTHOLOGY

# 26

# "The Map Is Not the Territory" and Biological Phases As Levels of Consciousness

*Biology Reflects Consciousness: Biological Changes Reflect Changes in Experience and Create the Spectrum of Consciousness*

## "The Stuff of the World Is Mind-Stuff"

We are living in stimulating and revolutionary times. For, even as we watch, the Newtonian-Cartesian paradigm is collapsing in the ocean of the new physics, "matter" is being swept away by "wavicles," and scientists are beginning to acknowledge what the poet-seers have always known: that physical reality is metaphor, that the external world and all of its components are subtle yet elaborate webs thrown upon the formless, meaningful forms created from no-thing-ness . . . that matter is metaphor for Consciousness — which is the only real stuff knowable about existence, in fact is the only stuff *of* the Universe.

129

Physicist and astronomer, Arthur Stanley Eddington (1928) phrased it: "The stuff of the world is mind-stuff." More recently, University of Minnesota physicist Roger S. Jones (1982) unveiled a position which he calls an "idealistic reevaluation of the physical world" (p. ix). He writes

*I reject the myth of reality as external to the human mind, and I acknowledge consciousness as the source of the cosmos. It is mind that we see reflected in matter. Physical science is a metaphor with which the scientist, like the poet, creates and extends meaning and values in the quest for understanding and purpose. (1982, p. ix)*

Even more recently, anthropologist Armand Labbe (1991) summed it up at a Society for the Anthropology of Consciousness conference saying, "Ultimately our physics . . . is going to demonstrate that essentially there is no such thing as matter. All there is, is mind and motion."

Granted, this is an extreme position, a strict Idealist stance. But it is the only truly supportable one, in light of what we know from the new physics. That would be enough in itself to cause us to reflect on it. But this perspective is also supported, even demonstrated, by the discoveries of the "new psychology" as well. More about that later.

It is ironic that it would be the most "materialistic" and "hardest" of the sciences that would be leading the charge against the primacy-of-the-physical-world postulate (and, unfortunately, leaving the rest of the sciences — both social as well as natural sciences — behind). The discoveries from quantum physics, though some of them almost a hundred years old now, are, only with difficulty, being assimilated into the other sciences. For the most part, they are largely ignored; science going along "as if" . . . that is, *as if* the Newtonian-Cartesian paradigm were still viable, *as if* the physical world was really "objective" reality, *as if* the mind could validly be considered an epiphenomenon of brain activity. So the old paradigm holds sway despite its inadequacy.

This is understandable, however. For truly acknowledging these newer perspectives requires a reformulation of theoretical positions, a rethinking of the Universe in much the same way that astronomical theories needed to be reformulated after the Copernican revolution. What we do not need are theories that disfigure themselves in trying to incorporate some (not all) of the new information and new perspectives in the way of the convoluted theories of the pre-Copernican astronomers who refused to accept the newer paradigm postulations.

This book, to the contrary, consistently presents a new-paradigm perspective.

In doing so it includes a rethinking of some theoretical constructions associated with Ken Wilber who, from this analysis, appears as inconsistent as pre-Copernican astronomers in devolving his theories.

## The Import and Consequences of the Primacy-of-Consciousness Postulate

It may also be argued that the new-paradigm primacy of consciousness is irrelevant to much of what is done in normal science. Whatever the truth of that, it must be acknowledged that theoretical positions that ignore the very foundations upon which they are based — that is, the subjectivity of the observer — are going to be weaker for that. Yet, acknowledging even that, one could argue that there is no clear idea of how to go about applying these new perspectives. How could they be used? How could they be relevant? What implications might they have?

It is in answer to these questions that I offer the following analysis of how these perspectives could be used in the understanding of child development. I propose a devolutional model — one that is rooted in Wilber's (1977) "spectrum of consciousness" theory. It is based also in the findings of new-paradigm experiential psychotherapies — that is, those that place primacy upon

131

experience over concept, "territory" over "map," and percept over object.

The implications of this approach, I hope to show, are for no less than the validity of the current direction of child-caring, the effectiveness of mainstream psychiatric approaches, and the direction of psychological and spiritual growth. It is my belief that such implications will not be considered to be irrelevant or unimportant; and I will deal with them at length in Part 3.

# Biology As Metaphor

At any rate, the knowable premise of the new science is that our physical world is a construction (of consciousness); that it can be metaphor, only, of the unknowable That Which Is; that, therefore, matter is metaphor. It follows that the sciences, which study this reflection of the unknowable Real, provide metaphors about metaphors.

## Moving in the Air Without Support

Schopenhauer saw it much the same way. His understanding of "ideas" is very close to what I am saying about science being composed of metaphors about metaphors. Gardiner (1966) explains this viewpoint of Schopenhauer:

*Schopenhauer distinguished a further class of ideas, namely, what he termed "ideas of Reflection," or sometimes "ideas of ideas" (Vorstellungen von Vorstellungen). It is in terms of these that we think about and communicate the contents of our phenomenal experience. In other words, they are the general concepts by virtue of which we can classify phenomena according to common features that are of interest or importance to us, forming thereby a conceptual structure or system which may be said to mirror or copy the empirical world. The function of this system is essentially a practical one; it provides a means of memorizing, and generalizing from, our observations of how things behave under varying conditions, and hence of putting to use what we learn from experience. Schopenhauer insisted, moreover, that this system cannot legitimately be separated from the foundation of empirical reality upon which it is based, and he claimed that concepts and abstract notions that cannot be traced back to experience are comparable to bank notes "issued by a firm which has nothing but other paper obligations to back it with." Consequently, metaphysical theories that pretend to offer an account of the world purely* a priori, *and that in doing so employ terms or propositions not susceptible to empirical interpretation, are empty of cognitive content; they "move in the air without support." (p. 327)*

In modern terms, "the map is not the territory" — the scientific construct is not the same as the experiential/empirical reality of existence; and the farther they are removed from each other, the more unsubstantial becomes the construct — ultimately collapsing of its own weight.

## Analyzing Scientific Dream-Weaving

Nonetheless, these metaphors — despite the threat of their moving "in the air without support" and cognizant of their practical value; these metaphors — because of the fact of their being for the empirical world a reflection or "mirror," which we then call "physical facts," "objective reality," or "scientific truths"; these metaphors can be analyzed in the same way that dream symbols are analyzed, that is, to uncover their deeper meanings.

Furthermore, this uncovering means essentially that we can discern their meanings for ourselves; "deeper meaning" being that understanding that relates the symbol to ourselves and that gives us understanding of our inner and outer actions and guidance for such behavior. In this way we can relate these "ideas about ideas," these scientific truths, back to our empirical, experiential, subjective reality . . . back to the base that they were originally the reflections and mirrors of. Thus we can come full circle, looking at ourselves from both inside as well as outside of ourselves and approaching, to the degree that a person can, a fuller understanding of ourselves and the world with which we are inseparable.

Specifically, then, for our purposes here, in looking at the biological sciences' metaphors of the human body — especially as concerns its structure, function, and ontogenetic and phylogenetic developments — we can discern and analyze an "underlying" meaning — a reflection of the Real, or of what Wilber (1977) calls Mind.

It is especially heuristic to analyze body for, as it has been said, body is concretized mind. This is not to mean concretized Mind — in Wilber's sense — but concretized ego (in the sense of the separate self, in the sense of mind as used by Sathya Sai Baba and other teachers who say that, ultimately, mind must be destroyed). Therefore, in contemplating the metaphors of the biological understanding of body, we can discern patterns and derive meanings concerning the separate self — its evolution, relationship to the whole, patterns of activity, stages of development, essence, and its experience of itself.

# Biological Phases As Levels of Consciousness

My attempt here is to skeletonize a portion of such an overall endeavor to show how it can be done and what kinds of meanings can arise. I will relate stages in the ontogenetic development of the human body to the dualities (splittings) of consciousness that, according to Wilber (1977), create the spectrum of consciousness.

Specifically, I will correlate the patterns of change in both form and experience (feeling) that a human undergoes with levels of consciousness. I will do this beginning with the sperm and egg; through the fetal, newborn, child, and adolescent forms; to the adult. What I am saying is that the forms that characterize the biological history of each individual (as delineated by the science of biology) and the processes that characterize the psychological history of each individual (as reported to us in the psychological sciences of the new experiential growth modalities) reflect, and correlate with, the changes in consciousness that Wilber describes as creating the spectrum of consciousness.

# 27

# Cellular Memory's Challenge to Materialism and Support for Panpsychism: Verifiable Memory of Events That Occurred Prior to Brain or Body Prove the Existence of "Spirit"

*The Body Arises from Consciousness, Not Vice-Versa, but There Is a Legitimacy to Heuristic Inquiry Into Form: The Epistemology Revealed by Cellular Memory*

## The Charge of Reductionism

Is this reductionistic? Am I saying that our ontogenetic development creates or causes the spectrum of consciousness? No. I no more mean that ontogeny creates the spectrum than that ontogeny creates phylogeny ... in that, as they say, "ontogeny recapitulates phylogeny."

One might deduce, however, that since this ontogenetic development, that is, this human prenatal development, is prior (in time) to the spectrum of consciousness that we observe and study in the Now, a cause-and-effect relationship is the most likely connection. But I must respond that this assumes the primacy of the physical form (in its ontogenetic development) over consciousness. This presupposition is, of course, a cornerstone of the Newtonian-Cartesian paradigm. Nevertheless, the very existence of consciousness or experience at the earliest levels I will be discussing (specifically, sperm, egg, zygote, and fetal) disputes the primacy-of-the-physical-universe postulate. To put it bluntly, consciousness can hardly be an epiphenomenon of brain activity if it exists when the brain does not.

Conversely, the body, brain, and cells cannot create the spectrum of consciousness for consciousness exists independent of them. The body reveals itself to arise from consciousness; it is the tip of the iceberg, which cannot be the foundation for the structures prior to or "below" or existing independently of it.

So the fact of memory and consciousness existing when the physical cells or the body cannot "create" them points inevitably to the primary reality/existence of something like Consciousness, Spirit, or Mind (or at least Energy) (see Adzema, 1985). Therefore, this type of impossible-to-have-existed-as-experience-or-to-be-existing-as-memory-according-to-the-N-C-paradigm experience can hardly be called the cause of the spectrum of consciousness. Indeed, something that cannot possibly exist within a paradigm can hardly be marshaled in to explain something within that paradigm.

However, if we accept the paradigm in which Consciousness, not form, is fundamentally real (which is exactly what we must do if we are going to look at evidence which supports, if not confirms, such a paradigm), and if we still want to accept the controversial concept of cause and effect, then the most we can really say is that prior experience of consciousness contributes to its later modifications. This perspective is certainly worthy of consideration.

# The Legitimacy of Heuristic Inquiry Into Form

But were it true that prior experience causes the later modifications of Consciousness (or as Wilber terms it, "Mind"), that truth is congruent with an analysis such as this one that considers form as to its metaphorical heuristic value in understanding experience and existence (or Mind, Consciousness) as it is immediately apperceived in the only Reality of Now. As Wilber (1977) makes adequately clear, from the only Real perspective of Here and Nowness, Absolute Subjectivity, or Mind, all "past" events are nonreal (that is to say, illusory) reflections of the Reality that is Now; they have no existence outside of this Now, so can hardly be called "causes" of Now.

From the perspective of Now, of Mind, of Absolute Subjectivity — which is the essence of the new paradigm — there is no cause and effect; there are only patterns of relationship existing Now. Hence these "prior" events are reflections of the immediate Reality, existing simultaneously in the Now as reflections, as metaphors. It is in this sense that they can be analyzed hermeneutically for their heuristic value in understanding the spectrum of consciousness as it arises this instant in the sole Eternal Moment.

# The Legitimacy of Cellular Memory

Despite what I have just said concerning the importance of an analysis of the biological metaphors of form — especially as they exist on the cellular level surrounding conception — as reflecting something of importance to us in a hermeneutic or heuristic sense, I want to at least put out a case for the legitimacy of cellular memory as something in its own right. That is, the rest of Part 2 will be based on a comparison of Wilber's spectrum of consciousness with the observable events and forms (the behaviors of the specific biological forms) as they are known to occur through the observational aspects of the science of biology. Still, the interpretation between the philosophical system and the biological form will be aided, supported, and fed by, among other things, the direct experience of memories of these states and forms, down even to the earliest, by myself and by the reports of such experiences by others.

So while this analysis does not stand on the absolute veracity of those experiences by myself or by others, still the analysis is certainly aided and helped by a belief in their legitimacy. I will say a few words about how memory can occur of such events, and more importantly, how that memory can be related to the foundations of our consciousness. A complete explanation (as I see it) of exactly this — that is to say, of how sperm and egg and zygote experience can lead to fundamental mythological, philosophical, and basic assumptions on the world, the self, and reality — can be found in two other works of mine (1981, 1984).

For our purposes here, let me just say that there are two possibilities that immediately come to mind: (1) what one might call the "prior conditions" theory and (2) Rupert Sheldrake's theory of morphic resonance and morphogenetic fields. Let us take them in turn.

# 28

# Morphogenetic Fields Theory Makes Genetics Obsolete and Unnecessary ... and Cellular Memory Understandable: The Theories of Morphic Resonance and "Prior Conditions"

*These Cellular Patterns Form Our Makeup, Our Thoughts,*
*Our Feelings, and Our Way of Viewing the World: The*
*Legitimacy of Cellular Memory*

## The "Prior Conditions" Theory

What I am calling the "prior conditions" theory is simply that the end result of any learning process, at any point, contains within it, if somehow broken down, all the prior conditions that produced it. It is based on the simple idea that the upper stories of everything will be in some way related to its foundation, and, more exactly, that the actual and specific foundation of anything can be exactly determined by reversing or tracing back in turn each step of its progression or building up.

Thus, this proposition states that all the experience, all the learning that occurs, is based upon prior learning and that all that comes about is in some way founded or based on stages that preceded that stage. The way this is understood to occur is in somewhat the same way that in a computer program a later stage necessitates a prior stage or as in any formal operation or in any learning at all later learning builds necessarily on particular prior understandings.

For example, in the case of learning a language: The speaking of a language requires at one point that the various sounds were learned, which requires that further back pronunciation of the various letters that make up the sounds were learned. Therefore, even though one may not retain a memory of learning the sounds and the individual letters, those events are encapsulated within the end result. Those prior stages had to have been there, and in some way are part of the construction of the end development; so much so that breaking down the end result leads necessarily to the factors of which it is composed.

This can be demonstrated in the case of computer programs and of codes of various kinds. Either of them, given sufficient analytical power (as we can now harness with the help of computers) and sufficient time can be broken down into their original constituents and into their necessary pattern of development. This being true — and allowing, this one time only, the dispensation of leaning on a physicalist presumption — since brains are seen as comparable in many ways to remarkably powerful computers, would it be so bold to assert that it might be possible for them to come up with its exact original conditions out of the current resulting conditions?

The prior-conditions theory is at least one possibility to explain cellular memory, then, and it is consistent with current psychological understandings of learning, development, and related processes.

Furthermore, this sort of process is also demonstrated in the phenomenon in psychology called regression. In these instances people will revert to earlier and earlier states of being, exactly as they were originally built up. They will often wear the same sorts of clothes, get the same illnesses, have the same intonations in their speech, and so on.

We see thus that each later stage contains within it all earlier forms, in some way. And that this is not dependent simply on some psychological memory mechanism is demonstrated by the fact that we observe the same phenomenon at work in the physical world in the form of the building up of multistory skyscrapers as well as that of multistep computer programs.

So in understanding cellular memory in this sense it is simply a matter of extrapolating our understanding of psychological regression much farther back than we are used to and adding the notion that from each successive stage can be accurately deduced its prior stages in turn, that the later stages could not be exactly as they are save for that the earlier stages happened to be exactly as they are. So this is one way of understanding how this memory could be contained in the adult range of experiential possibilities and how it could be legitimate.

# Morphogenetic Fields and Morphic Resonance

The other possible explanation, as I mentioned, is consistent with Rupert Sheldrake's (1981, 1991a, 1991b) theory. It can be stated this way: That concerning Sheldrake's morphogenetic fields, if things are done a particular way, they tend to be done that particular way in the future. He gives the example of ritual. A ritual is performed in the same way it has been for thousands of years, and there is a perceived potency in doing it that way in that there is somehow an accumulated power in each subsequent repetition of that act. He contends that somehow the field, the field of form, the morphogenetic field, is strengthened; the pattern is strengthened. Therefore when one re-enacts that pattern one is tapping into the field, via morphic resonance, that has been established.

Let us turn our attention now to thinking in terms of certain patterns that happen, for example, on the cellular level, to certain patterns that have been enacted for millennia. Keep in mind that Rupert Sheldrake's theory is not just concerning human beings and their thoughts and actions but applies also to all of Nature and the entire Universe. So there are morphogenetic fields acting on plants, for example, in the way that they produce the leaves of each individual plant. There is morphic resonance in all the patterns of Nature, even in the ways crystals develop. Thinking now in terms of the cellular level, human beings have been sperm and egg, have been fertilizing eggs for many millennia, have been sperm and eggs uniting the exact same way in conception for millions of years.

In fact many mammals reproduce exactly this way also. So, all told, there is a rather strong habit built up, a rather strong pattern that is a field that is of this pattern that exists in the Universe because of the repetition of this pattern over and over again in the Universe. So all of the aspects of sperm and egg experience — for example the experience of the sperm, that is, the struggle of the sperm — has been enacted practically an infinite number of times, more than can be imagined. For this is a strong morphogenetic field in the Universe, a strong morphic pattern. The point of all this is that since we resonate with things that are similar to us, and since a sperm is of a human being, then we would resonate with this pattern as we would resonate with this pattern of the egg and its experience or pattern. Likewise we would resonate with the pattern of conception itself and all that is subsumed under that, and afterwards also.

And of course all of the development of the fertilized egg and the blastocyst — the embryo and the fetus and all that — is part of a morphic pattern that is very well established. For our species it has been continuing practically an infinite number of times, having been enacted and being currently enacted, so that our species would find that this pattern would form part of our makeup, resonating with those patterns, and would form our thinking processes and feeling processes, and would help to structure our way of viewing the world and all else.

Finally the theory of morphic resonance states that we resonate with things with which we are more alike than not alike. Since we are more like ourselves than anything else, it follows that we would resonate more with our particular experience as a sperm and egg, for example, with its unique events, than with the experiences of other humans, or of other mammals or other species for that matter ... though those possibilities are not ruled out and in fact those kinds of events — trans-species sharing of experience of morphogenetic field — is actually reputed to occur at times (Grof 1976, 1980, 1985). At any rate, it is most likely we would resonate with and pick up on the field laid down by our own experience as such by our selves as an entity, as well as to a lesser extent resonating with and contacting the way it is done "in general," or "traditionally," by the species one belongs to. This also explains what in species other than our own is called instinct. It also makes understandable such remarkable patterns of behavior shared across generations, while genetic explanations, by contrast, appear rather preposterous.

Anyway, this is another way of looking at how these events at such an early level can actually influence the way we think, feel, and see the world, and how they can determine our basic assumptions about all of this.

# 29

# Mythology Tells the Tale of Our Lives as Cells: "Whatever Happened to Us in the Amnestic Years ... Is Projected Toward Cosmogony, Magic, and Other Human Beings"

*Our Myths Reveal Our Earliest Life, Going Back to Before Conception: Mytho-Empiricism and Our Devolution of Consciousness*

## Mytho-Empiricism and Biology As Mythology

Finally, mythology provides clues as to the events of these times. Shoham (1990) is one in particular who has made this case. Putting forth an approach at meaning which he calls "mytho-empiricism," he writes, "Mytho-empiricism is the utilization of myths not as illustrations of our theoretical premises but as their actual empirical anchors" (p. 34). He goes on to point out that scholars of myths have always regarded myths as reliable and faithful revelations of patterns of events that occurred prior to recorded history. Acknowledging that they can reflect patterns of events that are not otherwise accessible, he makes his case that the events that these myths are most actually reflecting are those of the earliest times in one's individual ... as opposed to cultural or collective ... life. Thus, he writes,

*Our methodological anchor . . . is the conception of myths as projections of personal history. Individuals are aware of their personalities as the sole existential entity in their cognition. Therefore, myths cannot be divorced from the human personality. This awareness of existence is the only epistemological reality. Whatever happened to us in the amnestic years and even later is projected toward cosmogony, magic, and other human beings. The events that happened in the highly receptive amnestic years have been recorded by the human brain. Events that happened after the amnestic years may be recalled cognitively, but whatever happened within these first years of life would be played back, inter alia, by myths of cosmogony. Myths as personal history may therefore be regarded as the account of some crucial developmental stages in the formative years. (1979, p. 21)*

## Correlation Between the Ontogenetic and the Phylogenetic

He notes that there is a correlation, however, between the early individual and the early historical events:

*Moreover, human development in the early formative years covers, in an accelerated manner, all the evolutionary phases of the species. Consequently, myths are also a projection of the development of the species as inherent in the development of the human individual. . . . That is, every human being experienced the Original Sin in his own development, so that the myth of the Fall is indeed a projection of an individual, yet universal, human developmental experience. (1990, p. 35)*

I point this out because while in this part — Part 2 — I will be using myths to indicate patterns of early individual events, in Part 3, I will bring them to bear as additional perspective on some of the early events of our species.

## Relative Universality of Myths Correlated With Importance in Ontogeny

Shoham (1990) qualifies his claims for the reliability of mythic projections by noting the obvious deduction that myths can vary in the degree to which they accurately project the common early experiences of the individual and that a good indicator of their reliability as regards universal patterns of early experience is the relative universality of the particular myth's appearance:

*Myths, however, become archetypal projections of human experience only when they are widespread. The more common a human developmental experience, the greater its chances of becoming a mythical projection. The inverse is also valid: the more widespread a myth, the greater the chances that it is a projection of a widespread or even universal phase of human development. The universality of the Fall myth, for instance, points to the fact that its corresponding developmental phase, the expulsion of the separate self from the pantheistic togetherness of early orality, is indeed experienced by every human being. (1990, p. 35)*

## Separant-Fusion Personality Dialectic

The personality theory derived from such a mytho-empirical base constructs the person as embodying two radically opposed tendencies — one the desire for fusion and the other for separation:

*Our personality theory envisages two core vectors, participation and separation. By participation, we mean the identification of ego with a person(s), an object, or a symbolic construct outside itself and the striving of the ego to lose its separate identity by fusion with this other, object or symbol. Separation is the opposite vector. These two vectors of unification-fusion and separation-isolation form the main axis of our personality theory. (Shoham, 1990, p. 33)*

## Stagelike "Degression"

It also puts forth a stagelike progression (or "degression"), created by these various earliest instances of separation or splitting off. The creation of these phases through splitting is remarkably like the creation of the spectrum of consciousness by the various splittings, creating the various dualities, that Wilber (1977) describes. The major difference is that Wilber's contention is the building up of these in the Sole Eternal Moment and Shoham's in the course of one's earliest existence ... Wilber's as creating the consciousness in the Moment and Shoham's as creating the personality. Shoham (1990) describes the progression:

*The first phase is the process of birth. The second phase is the crystallization of an individual ego by the molding of the "ego boundary." The third phase of separation is a corollary of socialization, during which, according to Erikson, one's "ego identity" is reached. (p. 33)*

And to these Shoham later adds a fourth.

# Stages Beginning at Conception, Not Birth

In the sections to follow, I will be presenting just such a progression, rather devolution, following the phases of early biological experience and correlating it both with the psychological development of the ego and personality development in general in a manner akin to Shoham's as well as to the building up of the spectrum of consciousness according to Wilber.

However, the major difference between my progression and Shoham's is that I start at conception as the first phase of separation and he starts at birth. In fact, I take Shoham's phases and place them one step back, so to speak. His birth scenario becomes what I see to be conception; his early orality phase, my phase of birth. At the third phase we begin to coincide in that both of our third phases coincide with the phase of socionormative indoctrination that reaches its peak at around the age of four. And finally our fourth stages are also identical in depicting the puberty or identity phase.

I make these differences from Shoham for compelling reasons. For one thing, what Shoham gives as an example of birth in mythology is actually much more like conception. It is so much more like conception that I feel he would also have placed it there if he had not, in following mainstream ego psychologists and outdated Freudian notions, been led to believe that neither consciousness or memory can exist from that far back. Therefore, I feel he makes this mistake only because he is operating on the basis of mainstream psychology and an outdated psychoanalysis that sees the beginnings of psychic life only at birth.

It is not surprising Shoham makes this mistake as it is only in the more recent field of pre- and perinatal psychology that we see the beginnings of psychic life going back into the womb and, in some understandings (including my own), to before conception. But with this understanding of where the beginning truly lies, his framework, his mythically expressed ontology, becomes strikingly fitted with the biological events. In altering Shoham's framework in this way, then, the following chapters will incorporate, for additional elucidation and perspective, the mytho-empirical light he sheds.

SECTION FIVE

# THE FIRST FALL FROM GRACE — SPERM/EGG AND CONCEPTION

# 30

Cellular Consciousness and the Chonyid Bardo: "Like a Prodigal Child, I Had Run Away from my Macrocosmic Home and Imprisoned Myself in a Narrow Microcosm" — Paramahansa Yogananda

*The Creation of Space, the Primary Dualism, and "the Appearance of Peaceful and Wrathful Deities"*

## First Fall From Grace

According to Wilber (1977), the *primary dualism* is the separation that first creates self and Other. Based upon both personal experience and study of several experiential growth modalities, I submit that this first fall from grace, the primary dualism, correlates ontogenetically with the phase of biological conception, more specifically with the creation of sperm and egg. Earlier I called this the *first shutdown*, which is the first time we have narrowed our consciousness, and I quoted Yogananda (1946),

153

"Like a prodigal child, I had run away from my macrocosmic home and imprisoned myself in a narrow microcosm" (p. 168).

Wilber (1977) describes the characteristics of the primary dualism: "This separation of subject from object *marks the creation of space: the Primary Dualism itself creates space*" (p. 120).

At the level of Mind, or Void, there is no form:

*The Absolute Subjectivity is sizeless or spaceless, and therefore infinite; but with the rise of the Primary Dualism, the subject is illusorily separated from the object, and that separation, that "gap" between seer and seen, is nothing more than space itself. Man, in identifying exclusively with his organism as separated from his environment, necessarily creates the vast and grand illusion of space, the gap between man and his world. (Wilber, 1977, p. 120)*

At the time of conception — specifically, with the creation of sperm and ovum — we have the emergence of form out of no-thing-ness (so to speak). That is, that there is the awareness of a separate thingness where before there was none. This awareness is referred to as cellular consciousness (Buchheimer, 1987; Farrant, 1987; Larimore, 1990a, 1990b; Larimore & Farrant, 1995). The memory we have of it is the earliest one we have of form within the frame of this particular physical form.

Cellular consciousness also relates to the beginnings of the *Chonyid bardo*, which, as described in the Tibetan Book of the Dead and reported by Wilber (1980, pp. 165-172), is a "period of the appearance of peaceful and wrathful deities" (p. 165). These appearances are caused by a contraction against the Clear Light, which transforms that Reality into "primordial seed forms of the peaceful deities (cf., Grof's BPM I level of experience in the womb) and these in turn, if resisted and denied, are *transformed* into the wrathful deities" (p. 165) (cf., Grof's BPM II and III levels of pre- and perinatal experience — but more about these processes in the next chapters). This is the time when — having missed the opportunity for mergence with the Clear Light during the Chikhai bardo, which occurs after death of the previous incarnation — one begins fleeing into form once again, attracted by the "impure lights" and "substitute gratifications" (p. 166).

That a separate consciousness exists here, at this cellular level, at least in the "reflections" that we call memory, is also evident in the research of psychedelics (Grof, 1976, 1980, 1985; Masters and Houston, 1967), in the memory retrieval acquired through hypnosis (Gabriel (1992); Wambach, 1979), and in the re-experience that occurs in experiential psychotherapy.[1]

# The Breaking of the Vessels and the Scattering of the Divine Sparks

Shoham's (1990) primary phase of separation is birth.

Nevertheless, with the additional perspective of pre- and perinatal psychology and of experiential psychotherapy we can add to and alter this formulation. Shoham writes, "In the first phase of separation, man is ejected from the comfortable womb and cruelly exposed to the elements in a manner that was recorded mytho-empirically in the Kabbalist catastrophe of the breaking of the vessels" (p. 35). Of course, I disagree with this. As stated at the beginning of this section, in the first phase of separation the individual leaves the godhead and generates form in the creation of sperm and ovum.

That the interpretation of the myth needs to be placed farther back in time, into the womb, is indicated even in Shoham's words, where he speaks of a "theurgic symbiosis and partnership between man and God" (p. 35). "Symbiosis" relates to the flow in < — > flow out feeling described as characterizing the BPM I or blissful womb state, that is to say, *before* birth. It is indeed correct to describe this time also as a "partnership between man and God" in that the fetus feels that all its needs are immediately responded to as well as it partakes of the emotional-psychic field of its mother (the experiential analogue of whom is "God").

# 31

## In the Beginning, the "Thin Pipe From Infinity … Emanated Light Into the World": We Begin with "Contraction" … Biological and Spiritual … How We Tell Ourselves That in Myth

*Divinity "Contracted Himself": "A Line Like a Thin Pipe Extended from Infinity to Create the Worlds."*

## The Thin Pipe From Infinity

Despite his placing the first separation at birth, Shoham (1990) does see that some elements of the mythic projection need to be interpreted farther back in time, into the intrauterine state. He writes,

*Before birth, there is the process of pregnancy and the formation of the human fetus to be considered. This, we claim, is depicted mytho-empirically by the Kabbalist dynamic of Tzimtzum (contraction). Rabbi*

*Haim Vital, the foremost disciple of Rabbi Isaac Luria and chief exponent of Lurianic Kabbala, describes the process of Tzimtzum:*

> *[Emanating Divinity] contracted Himself, a space round all around was formed. . . . After this contraction, a space was [thus] formed for emanant creatures to be created . . . and a line like a thin pipe extended from Infinity to create the worlds. . . . The pipe line created a round form . . . linked to the emanator (Infinity) by the pipe line only . . . and the line is thin so that it emanates light [livelihood] by measure and ration as needed by the emanant.*

*This would seem to be a plastic mytho-empirical depiction of the formation of the fetus within the round womb, fed by the umbilical cord stemming from an unknown emanator (to the fetus) in the away and beyond, perceived by the nascent awareness of the fetus and later projected onto mythology as Infinity. (1990, pp. 35-36)*

But we see indications going back still farther, to the time surrounding conception, in what Shoham presents here. The earliest events he cites are the formation of the fetus in the womb through the "thin pipe extended from Infinity to create the worlds." He claims this describes the situation of the fetus in the womb, being fed by the umbilical cord. However, with a slightly altered viewpoint on his depiction, his earliest events take on the characteristics of *the* earliest events, specifically, surrounding conception. This may be either an additional meaning to the myth or the more accurate meaning of the myth, however you choose to consider it (the multilevel quality of myths is well established).

At any rate, consider: In the process of contraction, *Tzimtzum*, there is this space in which things can be created. I have no quarrel with Shoham that the space described represents the womb. But there is this thin pipe from Infinity extended, the pipeline created around form, linked to the emanator by the pipeline only. Considering the near-universal relation of Infinity to the male (as contrasted with the similarly universal analogues of maternal to the manifest or temporal), I believe a masculine interpretation is warranted. You thus have a masculine Emanator Divinity contracting and being linked to this round place by a thin pipeline.

Then, right in the beginning, Divinity contracted himself. There's this round form linked to the emanator by the pipeline only. The line is thin so it emanates light, livelihood, measure, and ration as needed by the emanant; and it does so into the round place. A more accurate depiction of sexual intercourse and ejaculation from the viewpoint of the cellular would be hard to find.

There's a pipeline that's connected to "Himself" through which He emanates things out into the universe and creates them. According to the tradition, the line emanates light. Are these not the sperm coming out? The energetic sperm, biologically speaking, can be related to sparks of joy or sparks of life — as they have been described experientially.

Yet Shoham writes that this would seem to be a plastic mytho-empirical depiction of the formation of the fetus within the round womb during gestation. From this alternate perspective, however, the thin pipeline is not the umbilical cord. It emanates light from "Himself," the Father-God — who in reality is the father. Another way of saying: the father ejaculates sperm into the womb. Is not the inside of the penis, taking the sperm's perspective of course, also to be likened to a thin pipeline?

Shoham writes "fed by the umbilical cord stemming from an unknown emanator." I believe this is incorrect. This makes the "contraction" be the actual pregnancy; whereas the meaning of contraction is more accurately fitted to the processes, physically, of ejaculation on the part of the father and, spiritually, on the part of the newly created individual going from the Greater Reality into form.

# Divinity "Contracted Himself"

This is the actual coming into form of sperm and egg from undifferentiated reality and infinite potentiality; experientially, the self has "contracted."

It is also the first "split" — the first creation of something *Other* than One-Self.

So what I am proposing about the experiences surrounding conception, I contend, is a better analogue to the mythological Kabbalist depiction of *Tzimtzum*, contraction, and the thin pipe from Infinity, than is Shoham's interpretation of it as the umbilical cord and nourishment from the mother.

# 32

# The Scattering of the Divine Sparks and Divine Symbiosis: "Theurgic Conception"

*Before Conception, We Experience Omnipresence and Omnipotence, Knowing We Are Particles of Divinity. In the Womb, We Sense a Euphoric Symbiosis with the Divine*

## The Scattering of the Divine Sparks

Further support for this move in placing these interpretations farther back in time, to that of conception, is given by considering the Kabbalic mythical depiction of the breaking of the vessels and the scattering of the divine sparks. Shoham (1990) tells us,

*The myth of the breaking of the vessels relates to the birth-giving mother and the ejection from the womb, whereas the myth of the scattering of the divine sparks, which in Lurianic Kabbala occurs as a result, relates more directly to the neonate himself. The newborn child feels himself to be a precious particle of Divinity, omnipresent and hence omnipotent, because at this stage of his life he cannot be aware of anything or anybody except himself. (p. 36)*

In this way Shoham relates a myth of vessels breaking and a related myth of a scattering of divine sparks to the time of birth and the actual delivery. Contrary to what Shoham believes, I think the scattering of the divine sparks is a much more accurate depiction of what we might call "the scattering of the sperm." For it is always sperm that need to get scattered, widely dis*semin*ated, because they do not all survive. Fish fertilization, for example, involves male sperm being scattered over the top of the eggs.

Furthermore, "The newborn child feels himself to be a precious particle of Divinity" (p. 36). Regardless of the truth of that, more obviously we re-create the universe coming into form in the spewing out into form in an ejaculation: There are these hundreds of millions of "sparks" that go out from the father and each one of them is a precious particle of divinity in that each one could create the child.

Shoham adds, "Omnipresent and hence omnipotent because at this stage of life he cannot be aware of anything or anybody except himself." Once again, this does not fit with the later time of birth but with conception. For, as we see most clearly further on, at the time of birth and prior to it, the fetus is actually *distinctly* aware of an Other — distressingly and confrontationally so. Whereas around the time of conception there is that quality of omnipresence and omnipotence (more so at some times than others).

One has created form in the creation of sperm and egg, but one is only slightly removed from godhead; one still thinks oneself to be part of Everything.

# Divine Symbiosis

It is not until one gets farther along in the gestation process that one feels oneself to be truly distinct or is truly aware of the separation that has occurred. This happens with the encounter with the uterine wall during the latter stages of pregnancy. And yet Shoham, in referring to this time of breaking of vessels and scattering of sparks, uses the terms the "theurgic conception" of the Kabbala. He means this in a way much different than biological conception, yet I feel he may unconsciously have revealed the more accurate interpretation. It is interesting how the unconscious will lead us along, manipulating us to reveal the hidden truths, even in the very words that come to mind and despite our conscious intention in their use.

Further support for this interpretation occurs in his use of words after "theurgic conception," where he is overtly describing events occurring after birth. He writes, ". . . sees every human act as having an immediate effect on Divinity. This makes for a symbiosis between God and man." Once again, I believe he has covertly revealed the correct interpretation — in his use of the word *symbiosis* especially — that this is the time after *conception*, not after birth. During the intrauterine, post-*conception* time, there is exactly that quality of closeness to the Divinity. During this "BPM I" time, we have this dialectic going: this flow-in, flow-out between us and the universe, which is reflected physically (biologically) in the flow-in, flow-out between us and the mother through the umbilical cord.

# 33

# The Breaking of the Vessels and the First Separation: Mythology Supports What We Have Learned Experientially — The Release of Sperm and Egg Is the First Removal from Divinity:

*The First "Catastrophe" Is the Breaking of the Cellular*
*"Sisterhood" and the Release of the "Mongrel Hordes"*

## The Breaking of the Vessels

Shoham continues: "God needs man to 'mend' the catastrophe of the breaking of the vessels" (p. 36). By this he means that God needs man to mend the catastrophe of birth. He has told us that "The transition from the womb to the world outside is violent in all respects" and that "The shock of birth . . . is not remembered by us . . . but it is undoubtedly registered by our sub- or preconscious and is projected, *inter alia*, by myths" (p. 36). This fits exactly with our experiences and discoveries in the experiential psychotherapies.

## The First "Catastrophe"

But I disagree with his next statement: "The myth of the breaking of the vessels relates to the birth-giving mother and the ejection from the womb" (p. 36). The experiential psychotherapies tell us that birth is the second catastrophe and that the sense of catastrophe is associated initially with the time surrounding that of conception, with the first coming-into-form of sperm and egg.

With this in mind, the myth of the breaking of the vessels does not have to be related to the time of birth, for example, to the breaking of the mother's water; but can more accurately be situated, once again, farther back in time to that prior to conception. From this perspective the vessels that break are those of the testicles and the ovaries. The egg breaks free from the ovary; the sperm are suddenly released from the container of the testicles in an emission.

### The Cellular "Sisterhood"

It is known that the egg is inside of the ovary for the whole lifetime of the mother. The eggs are actually developed in the ovaries of the fetus; the girl about to be born has her eggs inside of her already. And at puberty her ovaries begin to release these eggs. She starts "breaking the vessels," so to speak. But the eggs have been there for a long time, sometimes going back twenty or thirty years. So by now a "sisterhood" has been created. Then what happens? At a certain point at the start of menstruation the vessels get broken, they start releasing eggs; before that they are sealed. Thus the "pact" between them (experientially speaking) is broken as well.

### The "Faceless Masses," the "Mongrel Hordes"

As for the male, the sperm are in the testicles a much shorter time. But the individual sperm are inside the testicle with hundreds of millions of other sperm. The testicle is also "sealed" until an ejaculation. One could think of that event as analogous as well to a breaking of the water before birth. The seal on that vessel has to be broken in order for the sperm to "spill" out.

## The First Separation, First Removal from Divinity

Thought of this way, the result of the breaking of the vessels — which Shoham says is the scattering of the divine sparks — is much more easily understood. Its interpretation does not have to be stretched to fit the idea of the sparks being the neonate itself. Rather the scattering-of-divine-sparks myth fits perfectly with the idea of the release of multitudes of sperm and egg upon the "breaking of the vessels" of the testicles and ovaries.

For these reasons I believe Shoham is wrong when he says this myth relates to birth; instead it relates to the experience of conception — lending support to the idea that conception is the first catastrophe, the first separation, the first removal from Divinity. Thus the myths support what we have discovered experientially at the level of cellular consciousness.

# 34

## "Mending the Catastrophe" … "Original Sin": The Child Is Tasked with Cleansing the World of a Taint Passed Down from the Beginnings of Time

*Collective and Ancestral Memory … "Original Sin": From the Perspective of Cells, Parents are "Blemished Gods" … For Parents, Children Are Their Immortality and Atman Projects*

## Mending the Catastrophe

To continue, Shoham writes that God needs man to mend this catastrophe of the vessels, and that this is part of the symbiosis, that this is part of what we are doing in our dialogue with the divine.

Considering my interpretation of the breaking of the vessels as the creation and release of the sperm and egg, we might say that the *mending*, then, of that breaking would be the sperm meeting the egg and the formation of a new union.

## Blemished Gods

But Shoham also talks about the God that is represented in these myths as being an imperfect God, a "blemished God." I will not go into his reasons for such an understanding. But consider that from the vantage point of the events surrounding conception this understanding of a "blemished God" fits as well: For when we are inside of our fathers and mothers and we are cells — either a sperm cell or an egg cell, either way — we are part of a being who is damn sure imperfect, acknowledged to be imperfect at that time. Partaking of our parents' beingness at that time, which both biologically and experientially is the case, we are identified with someone who is analogically Divine yet in their humanness is indisputably less than perfect — "blemished Gods."

## Children Are Parents' Immortality and Atman Projects

Furthermore, this ties in to what has been observed to be a primary and pervasive reason for parents having children. That is, parents want children in order to have a continuation of their selves. Essentially the child becomes the parent's "atman project" — that is, the continuation of the parent's attempt at perfection or of reuniting with or creating the lost and unconsciously yearned for state of divinity. A similar way of saying this is that children are parents' "immortality projects."

So, basically, children are released from parents, they "emanate" from parents, in order to try to mend what the parents feel themselves to have broken. The child represents the hope of the parent to be vindicated, completed; the chance for the adult to get it right, if not in his or her own lifetime, then at a time after one's death, through the actions of the biological being emanated from oneself.

Thus, in such mythology, God is very often accurately interpreted as the parent. What we have is a situation where children come out from the father and mother to try to mend their lives; so children are a continuation of the parents' (life) "project."

## Collective and Ancestral Memory

Shoham (1990) says further:

*This cosmic catastrophe gives Divinity a chance to cleanse him- or herself of his or her polluted components and allows man to save himself while mending the blemished divinity"* (p. 36).

Thus, a new conception, the creation of a new human life is felt to allow the parent to cleanse him- or herself of his or her polluted components.

But from the perspective of the newly created individual, this world scheme gives to humankind a chance to do better next time, to do better than the parent did, to overcome the "bad karma" of the parent that was put into the universe through that particular new form, that newly created being, and which originally is recorded in the sperm and in the egg. We, therefore, have here an indication of collective memories and pain as well as the hope of resolution of one's ancestral memories. This is to say that the child carries those things of its parents with it; and this world scheme gives the child a chance to cleanse the Divinity (the parent who by proxy represents the entire species and all progenitors) of its polluted components.

## "Original Sin"

This, then, is the child's chance to save itself; but the child is also coming into the world to help to cleanse the world of a taint that is passed down. It is an "Original Sin," so to speak, because its origins extend back through the generations in an infinite regress. Why the taint is there is a whole other question, however: It happens to be the focus of an entire other work of mine, *Planetmates: The Great Reveal* (2014).

## Duality and the Creation of Death

Nevertheless:

*According to the myth, the outcome of the breaking of the vessels was that particles of Divinity were imbedded in all objects and life-forms of creation, serving as divine cores within profane temporal casings. Furthermore, the breaking of the vessels introduced evil to the world; before, only good emanated from the great light of infinity. (Shoham, 1990, p. 36)*

In essence, then, as stated above, with the creation of sperm and egg we have the beginnings of form out of no-thing-ness. And with this creation, this first separation, evil has been created, darkness and confusion arise. For that separation is duality; and that duality is *evil* — the opposite of real life (God), *live* spelled backwards, and the beginning of the possibility of death.

# 35

# Womb with a View, the Transpersonal Bands of Consciousness: Womb Existence Is a Separate But Connected State, of Space But Not Time, an Eternal Now

*In This "Subtle Realm of Divine and Archetypal Illumination," Aware of Karma and Past Lives, We Are Instructed About Destiny and Life Purpose: the Chonyid Bardo, Womb, and Collective Unconscious*

## Transpersonal Bands: Womb With a View

At any rate, in that there is a separate awareness — in this creation of form, this creation of sperm and egg from no-thing-ness — there is a separation (of sorts) from the environment. But this separation is not total, not yet; there is a fluidity of awareness between environment and organism. Spiritually, it can be said that at this level one is still in touch with transpersonal forces or patterns.

These are Wilber's (1977) "transpersonal bands," which we see relate ontogenetically to the time in the womb.

## Chonyid Bardo, the Archetypal Realm, the Womb, the Collective Unconscious

They relate also to the later stages of the Chonyid bardo which, as Wilber (1980) writes, is "the subtle realm of divine and archetypal illumination" (p. 169). The separation from Other at this level takes global, archetypal, karmic forms. One is "instructed" about destiny, life purpose, and so forth; one's karmic and past lives patterns are still very much "at hand." This is Masters and Houston's (1967) *symbolic level*, Jung's collective unconscious, and Grof's transpersonal realms.

## Separate But Connected State

Biologically, emotionally, and psychically, the organism is also connected to its "environment." After the sperm and ovum unite to create the fertilized egg, it grows into a blastocyst and implants itself in the uterine wall. Later as fetus, of course, it shares in the mother's biological processes and substances through the umbilical cord. So the organism here is actually still "attached" to its environment, though maintaining a separate awareness, an awareness of space.

Wilber's primary duality has occurred, which for our purposes might be described as the separation between self and Other or self and God. The heavens have been separated from the earth, though they still meet at the ends of the horizon. Throughout its time in the womb the organism is attached to the mother (the environment) and shares freely in her feelings, thoughts, moods, and energies. It is a vegetative-type existence, separate yet connected.

## Space Without Time — The Womb's Eternal Now

This is the condition of space without time. This womb period has retained timelessness but not space- or formlessness. One lives an eternal Now that is rooted in a specific form — that is, it has a specific perspective or focal point of awareness.

Note that, contrary to Wilber's (1977) assertion, the primary and secondary dualisms — those which create space and time, respectively — do not occur together when looked at ontogenetically. This difference from Wilber is significant, and I shall discuss it further on. For present purposes, however, remember that Wilber's secondary dualism creates a past and future, which place a veil between us and Now. But on the contrary, at this point in the womb, death has not yet entered the picture and time has thus not been generated nor, consequently, a past and future. We therefore have the continuing sense of eternity and of the immortality of form.

## End of Innocence — Birth

But something does happen (according to biologists, pre- and perinatal psychologists, and the reports of experiential pioneers). This leads us to the second fall from grace, to the experience of birth.

SECTION SIX

# THE SECOND FALL FROM GRACE — BIRTH

# 36

# The Beginnings of Diminishing Divinity and of Our Becoming Just an Idea: We Create Time to Escape from an Insufferable Now ... Therein We Create Death

*The Wall: The Creation of Pain, Time, and Death Occurs with the Encounter with the "World-Obstacle"*

## The Secondary Dualism

Ontogenetically, the second fall is birth and correlates with Wilber's secondary dualism, which he relates to the creation of time. As Wilber (1977) puts it, "the *why* of time's genesis . . . it is nothing other than man's *avoidance of death*" (p. 120).

He continues as follows, quoting Benoit (1955):

*It is with the arising of the Existential Level that there occurs the infamous debate of "to be or not to be;" because at the moment man severs his organism from his environment, then*

> *Suddenly he becomes conscious that his principle is not the principle of the universe, that there are things that exist independently of him, he becomes conscious of it in suffering from contact with the world-obstacle. At this moment appears conscious fear of death, of the danger which the Not-Self represents for the Self. (1977, p. 122)*

## The Creation of Death in Encounter with the World-Obstacle

We see that fear of death arises out of suffering from contact with the world-obstacle. The metaphorical reflections of this, biologically, are the fetus's encounter with suffering in the later stages of pregnancy. The fetus encounters the "world-obstacle," the uterus, with the confinedness in the womb and its attendant suffering increasing daily and hourly. The fetus becomes even more conscious of this obstacle — and more identified with its physical form — in reaction to the Energy eruption from frustration.

# The Wall

So it is here farther along in the gestation process that we feel the separation (from divinity) with the encounter with the wall of the uterus. People use that metaphor: "I hit the wall." In other words, "I've reached my limit." This harkens back to that time in the womb.

Shoham (1990) writes, "In the midst of his omnipresent egocentricity, he experiences disastrously hostile surroundings" (p. 36). Though Shoham likens this to the "expulsion" phase of birth, this experience actually begins a little earlier, during the BPM II phase of birth — that is, in the late stages of pregnancy prior to the onset of labor.

Let me clarify this. With the primary split, occurring with the creation of sperm and egg from no-thing-ness, one's intention can be different from the intention of Other. Indeed, one perspective on this is that a difference in intention *causes* the creation of sperm and egg — that is, the foundation of the world is wrought of an initial rebellion from God.

Regardless, up until this point in the developments prior to birth, these two intentions have rarely been at odds: The self's intentions to grow and to expand have been nurtured and aided, in a wonderfully synchronistic way, by the Other — in this case, specifically, by the environment of the mother's body.[1]

Toward the end of pregnancy, however, the organism's intentions to grow and expand are contrary to the environment's intentions to resist *its* further growth in response. By this I mean simply that there are limits to the elasticity of the womb and the mother's body, which result in its becoming an increasing contrary pressure against the fetus's growth. To the fetus, however, with the possibility of a different perspective — a "bi-focal" world arising with the primary split — it is as if the environment has "turned against" or "betrayed" it.

At any rate, this friction of opposing intentions (or perspectives) is Energy, just raw Energy until it is labeled. As Wilber (1977) put it:

*As an example of this entire movement, let us again use the mobilization of anger, as when a person strikes me. The actual strike itself, in its simplest form, is just a movement of the universe, but as the primary dualism starts to occur, I sense a mobilization of energy arising within me. At this stage — before the primary dualism hardens — this energy is still pure, informal, intemporal. . . . (p. 190)*

## The Creation of Pleasure and Pain

In our example, of course, it is not someone striking the fetus. It is someone opposing the fetus's uninhibited growth. The pattern is the same, however, in that "in its simplest form" the actual blocking of the fetus's free movement "is just a movement of the universe."

However, then the fetus does what indeed we all did. Since we were not "wholly" enough to accept this pure energy as simply *our* energy, our divinity (the consequence of the primary split), we make it "wrong," we "label" it pain. This, of course, is not conceptual labeling here since concepts do not exist as yet. Rather, it is pure, organismic avoidance/rejection . . . a kind of cosmic mistrust.

Nonetheless, in "labeling" this confinedness in the womb, or "walling-in," as "wrong" we seek to escape from it into a world of "right." Therefore, out of the original creation of self and Other or organism and environment — with its concomitant of organism and obstacle (world-obstacle) — we have created the splitting of primary Energy into energy inside and energy coming from outside, into right and wrong, and therewith, pleasure and pain.

## We Create Time to Escape from an Insufferable Now

Furthermore, since we cannot escape pain into space (we cannot move away or out . . . yet), we create another duality: the duality of time — of past and future. The fetus, in that time prior to birth ("up against the wall"), seeks to escape into memories of a sweetness just recently removed. With this move we have created the duality of life and death, of being and nonbeing. We have created nonbeing in that we are trying to escape the Now into the past which is a mere memory, an *Idea*, a reflection only of the Now. Herein we have the beginnings of becoming just an idea.

# 37

# Becoming Separated from Our Bodies at Birth, We Are Separated from Archetypal and Karmic Patterns, from Our Spiritual Selves: An Angel of Death Guards the Gates of Heaven

*The Creation of Ego: There Is a Separation from the Natural and the Institution of a Substitute Human Nature at Birth*

Grof (1976, 1980, 1985), in his many works, describes vividly this creation of death at the time of birth. His growth modality, called holotropic breathwork, uncovers conscious and palpable awareness of death alongside the agonies of birth in thousands of participants and thereby demonstrates their interconnectedness. Similarly, Janov (1983) points out that for many of us the time of birth is the closest we come to death for our entire lifetime, until of course our actual physical demise.

In reliving their births, participants gasp for air, turn red, scream, struggle fiercely — exhibiting to all about the terror of death and the titanic will to survive . . . being versus nonbeing. But the neonate cannot escape into space, and is only little able to escape into time.

Therefore, as Wilber (1977) put it:

*In fleeing death, man is thrown out of the Now and into time, into a race for the future in an attempt to escape the death of the timeless Moment. The Secondary Dualism-Repression-Projection, because it severs the unity of life and death, simultaneously severs the unity of the Eternal Moment; for life, death, and eternity are one in this timeless Now. In other words, the separation of life and death is ultimately and intimately the same as the separation of past and future, and that is time! Hence is the Secondary Dualism the progenitor of time. And this means that the life in time is the life in repression, specifically, the Secondary Repression. (p. 124)*

Similarly:

*Man's flight from death also generates the blind Will to Life, which is actually the blind panic of not having a future, the panic that is death. . . . Under the anxiety of fleeing death, the life of the organism itself is severed, its unity repressed and then projected as a psyche vs. a soma, as a soul vs. a body, as an ego vs. the flesh. (p. 124)*

Further on:

*Man, not accepting death, abandons his mortal organism and escapes into something much more "solid" and impervious than "mere" flesh — namely, ideas. Man, in fleeing death, flees his mutable body and identifies with the seemingly undying idea of himself. Corrupt but flattering, this idea he calls his "ego," his "self." (p. 125)*

Joseph Chilton Pearce (1980) describes this separation from the natural and the institution of a substitute "human nature" at birth in this way:

*Future historians will shudder in loathing and horror at the hospital treatment of newborns and mothers in this very dark age of the medicine man and the surgeon and their uses of chemicals and cuttings. (p. 44)*

*The aftereffects of technological hospital delivery are permanent. We have built an elaborate body of knowledge not only rationalizing the damage we have done, but also accepting the damaged product as natural and inevitable. And we accept all the massive problems resulting as "human nature." (p. 45)*

Having severed its self from its body — the metaphorical reflection of which, from a physical perspective, is the actual separation of mother and child at birth with the severing of the umbilical cord — the newborn has severed itself from its archetypal and karmic patterns, its relation to the Universe, its innate destiny and purposiveness. These realities lie ever afterwards out of reach on the other side of death.

Should there come a time in adulthood when the ego seeks intentionally to retrieve them, they will await a confrontation. They will be released only upon the acceptance, reliving, and integration of that darkest face from which one has flown . . . whether that integration be a holotropic death-birth experience, a primal-like reliving of birth trauma, a mystic dark night of the soul, a descent into hell or journey to Hades, the crucifixion/ego-death/ resurrection scenario of a benign psychotic "break," or a worked-through "spiritual emergency."

However, this idea of ego into which one has fled is at this point newly formed and empty. An empty vessel or blank slate, it is ready to be filled with the contents of or written on with the concepts of culture. Dependent and helpless in its doubly separated state, it is eager now to mold and shape its newly created sense of self — as idea, as ego — with whatever patterns of experience present themselves. Buoyed up by concept against the tide of death's muted presence, the ego is eager to fortify itself . . . for the smell of darkness is still close; the echoes of hell too recent.

This then is what remains of Energy, of Mind, of Absolute Subjectivity, of God. An angel of death guards the gates of heaven.

# 38

## The Creation of Loneliness and the Expulsion from Paradise at Birth: The Why and Way of Mind, or Ego, Separating from Universal Consciousness

*Ejection from "Eden" Happens to Everyone at Birth:*
*Suffering Builds a Character*

Shoham (1990) provides additional light on this second phase of separation. As mentioned previously, he relates the second phase of separation to that between early and later orality during the toddler stage of development (approximately age two to three). And I repeat here again that his second phase appears instead to fit more perfectly with the phase of separation at birth.

Shoham notes, first of all, that the second phase of separation involves being ejected from "pantheistic togetherness" and that it is related to the mythical "expulsion from paradise" (p. 36). Considering what has been said so far and what is known about the experience of being in the womb and of being born (for example,

BPM I, followed by BPM II and BPM III — in Grof's [1976, 1980, 1985] terminology), it should be clear how the experiential and mythical components Shoham cites relate to the experience of birth.

Furthermore, he writes that this expulsion from paradise "sees God condemning man to a cursed land in which he will live in sorrow all his temporal life" (p. 36). This statement expresses, indeed, the consequences of birth pain on a person's life. However, his statement that "the pantheistic neonate learns through deprivational interaction . . . that he is not with everything but against everything" (pp. 36-37) is not quite true. It is not through *deprivational* interaction (not yet, anyway) but through *confrontational* interaction with the uterus in the manner previously described that the neonate first learns such a hard lesson. But, surely enough, as Shoham then points out, this event "gives way to the loneliness and encapsulated existence of the human individualized *separatum* " (p. 37).

The upshot is that we become separated at birth; at birth a second duality arises in us. "This separation," like the earlier separation in the creation of sperm and ovum, "is also perceived by the organism as a catastrophe" (Shoham, 1990, p. 37). It is coupled with a transition from grace in the womb "to the harshness of temporal stern judgment" (Shoham, 1990, p. 37). For *stern judgment*, read *birth*.

Why is birth "stern judgment"? It is so because something happens in the womb that is with us for the rest of our life. This coming up against the uterine wall is seen as a judgment by the fetus. I will explain why in a little bit.

First, let me point out Shoham's statement "the light of Infinity was boundless, eternal, imperceptible, and nondifferentiated" before creation (p. 37). Furthermore: "The motivation of the emanating Infinity in forming separate entities was to be able to confer grace on them" (p. 37). This makes sense, "because within the unity of Infinity there can be no giving and no receiving" (p. 37).

Therefore, one has to have an Other in order to have the joy of flowing in and flowing out. There was no flow-in, flow-out prior to the time of the creation of form.

However, Shoham claims that "the differentiation of the emanant is effected by its swallowing of harsh *Dinim* (stern judgments)" (p. 37). So originally, after the creation of sperm and egg, after the creation of form, the "differentiation" — that is to say, the continued elaboration of form, of the individual — is brought about by the encounter with stern judgments. On the adult level, we would say "suffering builds character."

But on the prenatal level, this means that after the original duality there is the continued possibility, not only for there to be giving and receiving (flowing in, flowing out), but for there to be differences in intention between the self and the Other. And it is through the successive encounters with these differences or frictions of intention that the organism is stimulated to differentiate. In other words, the prenatal organism must grow in order to survive (see Adzema, 1994b).

More and more the fetus comes up against "harsh reality" and this causes it to become more and more differentiated, to become more and more complex and less and less unitary. The prenatal penultimate of this occurs, as mentioned, in the final stages of gestation in the fetus's coming up against the resistance of the womb, which results in a *major* differentiation or complexity — the creation of another duality. But all along, as well, there have been the "swallowings" of harsh *Dinims* that have resulted in differentiation and increased complexity: the incompleteness and inferiority feelings of the sperm and egg (they have only half the number of chromosomes, after all) leading to the need to unite, the "survivor guilt" of the fertilized egg leading to cell multiplication, and the foundationlessness of the blastocyst leading to the need to implant in the uterine wall (see Adzema, 1994b).

Yet for this entire time in the womb, while there are obstacles, there are also ways around them, not to mention the experience of grace all about (being synchronistically nurtured by the womb). It is akin to a stream flowing downhill, over and around rocks and debris; no stopping it. As a fetus, one's intention is to grow and grow and grow. So you're expanding, you're becoming blissful — you're "blasting, billowing, bursting forth with the power of ten-billion butterfly sneezes." Then all of a sudden: Boom! You hit a wall. Now there is no bubbling blissfully over it, no courseway around it; no exit.

It is felt as a stern judgment: "What did I do wrong?" And this causes one to differentiate more. You no longer say: "Wow, I'm the whole universe." Now you have to say: "I'm not what I thought I was." This is the incipient ego talking. In a way, there is fear: there is this "aggressor" (the womb); you have to "defend" in a way. And the beginnings of defenses is most accurately the beginnings of ego and of ego boundary.

# To Summarize

To summarize, "The breaking of the vessels generated vileness in divinity and then vicariously in creation" (Shoham, 1990, p. 40). That is, the creation of sperm and egg created the possibility of corruption, of difference in intention from that of the divine. That is the beginning of evil. Then, "the expulsion of man from pantheistic paradise, resulted in the creation of the first human polar archetypes" (p. 40). So with birth there is the creation of the first polar archetypes — the creation of past and future, space and time, and birth and death.

In such manner, then, are the patterns of ego and "mind" separated and severed from underlying and forgotten (but not *unfelt*) patterns of archetypal, karmic, psychic, and universal self existing as body.[2]

The newly emergent conceptual bank is ripe for the impressions of society and culture, hence, the emergence of the biosocial bands.

# 39

# Becoming Not Yourself: The Centaur Stage of Infant and Toddler Learning Involves Learning You Are Not OK and Continues the Separation from Innate Divinity

*The Newborn Is the Centaur — Half Human, Half Animal ... Half Human, Half Divine: The Biosocial Bands ... The Cultural Veil*

## Biosocial Bands: The Cultural Veil

### A Vast Screen That We Throw Over Reality

Most importantly, these biosocial bands are the postnatal, infantile, and early childhood experiences. Wilber (1977) has a narrower conceptualization of them, yet his elaboration still holds:

*The Biosocial Band, as the repository of sociological institutions such as*

187

*language and logic, is basically, fundamentally, and above all else a matrix of distinctions, of forms and patterns conventionally delineating, dissecting, and dividing the "seamless coat of the universe."*

*Thus the Biosocial Band, if it isn't directly responsible for all dualisms, nevertheless definitely reinforces all dualisms, and so perpetuates illusions that we would ordinarily see through. . . . The Biosocial Band, as a matrix of distinctions, is thus like a vast screen that we throw over reality. (p. 135)*

## Biosocialization: Nursing and Nurturing Events Create Templates for Later Language and Logic

Language is important in structuring experience, as well as are all the other factors of socialization alluded to by Wilber above, but the fundamental biosocialization occurs at the mother's breast, so to speak. Postnatal hospital experiences and nursing experiences are foremost events in the structuring and patterning of all later form, including that of language and logic. Later on, weaning, toilet training, and other infant and early childhood experiences have secondary but still immensely strong influences in shaping the very way that reality is perceived and reacted to.

# The Cultural Veil

However, compared to earlier (biological and biocultural) experiences, these postnatal experiences are heavily culture-rooted. Therefore they are hugely variable. And they in turn serve eventually to shape the exoteric contents of culture. This is to be contrasted with biocultural influences at the transpersonal bands, the womb level, where (relatively) universal biology makes for relatively universal patterns and structures.[3]

## This Postnatal Body-Ego Is "Animalian" Compared to "Vegetative" in the Womb

At birth we have the beginnings of the idea that is the ego. But Wilber (1977) points out this is initially a body-ego. Therefore, if the womb could be called vegetative, this state of body-ego could be called animalian. The child is severed from direct transpersonal access, but these realities exist as bodily felt feelings. Through the emergence of the biosocial bands, however, that sense of bodily and transpersonal awareness is increasingly replaced with ego consciousness and consciousness of cultural form.

## The Centaur Is the Toddler — Half Human, Half Animal … Half Human, Half Divine

So this initial socialization is patterned upon a foundation of bodily feelings (which are themselves the remnants of transpersonal realities). Thus, it is fitting that the symbol Wilber (1977) uses is the Centaur — half human, half animal — the conceptual, cultural, "civilized" portion melded, as it were, to the remnants of transpersonal reality, which at this point are only experienced as bodily pushes and pulls, patterns of feelings, "instincts."[4]

## The "Primal" Person Is to Cycles of Nature as the Baby Is to Mother's Routines for Caring

The relation to transpersonal realities here is far from identification. We talk instead of attunement to cosmic rhythms or living in accordance with natural cycles. For the "primal" or "archaic" person (the person of pre-history), these rhythms may be seasonal and related to agricultural processes and cycles of nature and time. For the young child, these rhythms are biological and cultural. The newborn must find a way to strike a balance between its own cycles of hunger, thirst, sleep, defecation, play, and needs for touch and affection, and the cycles of its caretaker — whose rhythms, even under optimal conditions, are not going to synchronize with the newborn's as perfectly as was the case in the womb.

# Becoming Other Than "I"

This tension, then, pushes the emergence of the biosocial bands. For with the passage of time this discrepancy widens. At first an attempt is made to cater to the newborn's rhythms. But more and more the infant is required to conform to external cycles: from feeding on demand to on a schedule, from nursing to weaning . . . eventually there is toilet training. At each stage the child is told, in unmistakable ways, that he or she is not okay the way that she or he is, that she or he must conform to outer patterns. This continues throughout the infant and toddler years until the age of about four or five.

## Learning to Forget and Forgetting How to Feel

Thus, this process of layering of bands of biosocial learning — of learning to forget and forgetting how to feel one's inner pushes, pulls, and feelings — widens, with each new repression, the wall between self and divinity. And this depiction characterizes the state from birth on and through the infant and toddler years. It extends up until the time of another, even greater, separation — another major splitting or fall from grace, the creation of another major duality in consciousness. This phase occurs around the age of four or five and is called by Arthur Janov (1970) the *primal scene*.

# SECTION SEVEN

# THE THIRD FALL FROM GRACE — THE PRIMAL SCENE

# 40

## At the Age of Four or Five, Giving Up, We Become "Them": Life Is Passed Performing Rituals and Mouthing Incantations in the Service of Others' Requirements

*The Natural Self Slain, the Ego "Is Rewarded for Being Obsequious While the Real Self Seethes in the Prison of Loneliness": "Child Sacrifice"*

## The Primal Scene

The primal scene occurs at around the age of four or five years. It corresponds exactly with Wilber's tertiary dualism, as also it correlates with the beginning of the Oedipal struggle (in Freudian terms). It consolidates the formation of the ego against the body, severing the Centaur into "a horseman divided from his horse" (Wilber, 1977, p. 149). It may be likened to a *third shutdown*, a third stage in the removal of self from divinity, a third denial of

God — this time under the terrorizing influence of what might be called social or relationship trauma.

## The Natural Self Is Slain

According to Arthur Janov (1970), at around the age of four or five there occurs a point at which the child perceives the hopelessness of ever being loved for him- or herself and becomes instead what the parents (and, by proxy, society) want. Their needs become her or his needs.

The real self — the "child within," the natural self, the God within — is slain and buried in the unconscious (once again) and becomes the unconscious self. Janov (1970) explains this process of losing the real self in a systematic and detailed manner. He writes brilliantly and poetically in his description, and I will let his words do most of the talking here.

Janov points out, first of all, that

*We are all creatures of need. We are born needing, and the vast majority of us die after a lifetime of struggle with many of our needs unfulfilled. These needs are not excessive — to be fed, kept warm and dry, to grow and develop at our own pace, to be held and caressed, and to be stimulated. These Primal needs are the central reality of the infant. The neurotic process begins when these needs go unmet for any length of time. . . .*

*Since the infant himself cannot overcome the sensation of hunger (that is, he cannot go to the refrigerator) or find substitute affection, he must separate his sensations (hunger; wanting to be held) from consciousness. This separation of oneself from one's needs and feelings is an instinctive maneuver in order to shut off excessive pain. We call it the split. (p. 22)*

The split evolves into the permanent disconnection between the real and the unreal selves — between the real, needing, "feeling" self and the self we must pretend to be in order to try to get some our needs satisfied.

*Demands for the child to be unreal are not often explicit. Nevertheless, parental needs become the child's implicit demand. The child is born into his parents' needs and begins struggling to fulfill them almost from the moment he is alive. He may be pushed to smile (to appear happy), to coo, to wave bye-bye, later to sit up and walk, still later to push himself so that his parents can have an advanced child. As the child develops, the requirements upon him become more complex. He will have to get A's, to be helpful and do his chores, to be quiet and undemanding, not to talk too much, to say bright things, to be athletic. What he will not do is be himself. The thousands of operations that go on between parents and children which deny the natural Primal needs of the child mean that the child will hurt. They mean that he cannot be what he is and be loved. . . . (p. 25)*

# Becoming "Them"

The upshot of this process, then, as Sam Keen (1972) described it:

*He knows he cannot both be himself and be loved. So he splits into a real and an unreal self. His real feelings are sealed in the throbbing vault of the lonely inner self and he begins to tailor his conduct to the expectations of his parents. His watchword becomes: I will be what you want me to be if you will only love me. Although I feel hurt, alone, fearful, and unlovely, I will act trustworthy, loyal, helpful. . . . Henceforth the budding neurotic child gets plastic approval but no genuine love. His unreal self is rewarded for being obsequious while his real self seethes in the prison of loneliness. (p. 46)*

## Body Snatchers

The *primal scene* itself, however, is that crystallizing event that for the child symbolizes the essential truth of all the accumulated interactions that from birth on have demonstrated that in order to get a semblance of one's needs fulfilled one cannot simply be oneself but must instead struggle to please another — for now a parent or parents, later it will be a lover, a spouse, a boss, society in general.

## Giving Up, We Become "Them"

Janov (1970) describes this primal scene:

*As the assaults on the real system mount, they begin to crush the real person. One day an event will take place which, though not necessarily traumatic in itself — giving the child to a baby sitter for the hundredth time — will shift the balance between real and unreal and render the child neurotic. That event I call the major Primal Scene. It is a time in the young child's life when all the past humiliations, negations, and deprivations accumulate into an inchoate realization: "There is no hope of being loved for what I am." It is then that the child defends himself against that catastrophic realization by becoming split from his feelings, and slips quietly into neurosis. The realization is not a conscious one. Rather, the child begins acting around his parents, and then elsewhere, in the manner expected by them. He says their words and does their thing. He acts unreal — i.e., not in accord with the reality of his own needs and desires. In a short time the neurotic behavior becomes automatic.*

*Neurosis involves being split, disconnected from one's feelings. The more assaults on the child by the parents, the deeper the chasm between real and unreal. He begins to speak and move in prescribed ways, not to touch his body in proscribed areas (not to feel himself literally), not to be exuberant or sad, and so on. The split, however, is necessary in a fragile child. It is the reflexive (i.e., automatic) way the organism maintains its sanity. Neurosis, then, is the defense against catastrophic reality in order to protect the development and psychophysical integrity of the organism.*

Neurosis involves being what one is not in order to get what doesn't exist. *If love existed, the child would be what he is, for that is love — letting someone be what he or she is. Then, nothing wildly traumatic need happen in order to produce neurosis. It can stem from forcing a child to punctuate every sentence with "please" and "thank you," to prove how refined the parents are. It can also come from not allowing the child to complain when he is unhappy or to cry. Parents may rush in to quell sobs because of their anxiety. They may not permit anger — "nice girls don't throw tantrums; nice boys don't talk back" — to prove how respected the parents are; neurosis may also arise from making a child perform, such as asking him to recite poems at a party or solve abstract problems. Whatever form it takes, the child gets the idea of what is required of him quite soon. Perform, or else. Be what they want, or else — no love, or what passes for love: approval, a smile, a wink. Eventually the act comes to dominate the child's life, which* is passed in performing rituals and mouthing incantations *in the service of his parents' requirements. (pp. 25-26,* emphases mine*)*

## In Myth: Isaac's "Primal Scene"

A good mythic reflection of the dynamics of this third fall from grace is the Abraham and Isaac story in *Genesis*. In the story, God "tempts" Abraham by telling him to sacrifice his only son, Isaac. Therefore, the altar Isaac is to be sacrificed on is that of the parent's own misapprehended growth needs.

## What Is Meant by "Child Sacrifice"

Moreover, just as Isaac, the son, the child, is to be offered in sacrifice to Abraham's relationship to the divine, to his supposed spiritual needs; so also we, most of us, are asked to forego our own dreams, our own unique directions, for the unfulfilled dreams, desperate hopes, and ego vanity of another — usually the same-sex parent.

# 41

## Having Become "Them," We Are Left Forever Asking "Who Am I?" ... The Philosophic Bands

*If Not My Self, Who Then to Be? Surrendering One's Natural Self and Imprisoning Divinity in a Pandora's Box Within, One Is Plagued with Wondering Who to Be*

## Philosophic Bands: Who to Be?

After the consolidation of the ego, the unreal self, at the primal scene and its consequent severing of even the *felt* connection to transpersonal realities by way of the body through severance of ego from body, one is no longer concerned with addressing one's reality (in terms of attempting to secure even the satisfaction of felt needs).

Since one has given up on being one's self, all that remains is to decide *who to be*. In the struggle to decide *who to be* (in order to be loved), we have the emergence of the philosophic bands.

## Driven by Needs for Acceptance, Belongingness, Self-Esteem Rooted in Our Personal "Big Bang"

Their emergence is pushed by the force of unmet needs, which at this point stem most immediately from needs for simple acceptance, belongingness, self-esteem; but farther back have roots in the energy of unmet biological needs at infancy and early childhood; in the repressed dynamo of the fear of death inherent in the birth trauma; in the energy of unaddressed transpersonal yearnings and directives; all the way back in the energy of the original act of creation of the primary dualism (the creation of sperm and ovum, of form out of no-thing-ness) which, from this perspective on the other side of all the subsequent blockages and repressions of Energy, is beginning to look like some kind of "big bang."[1]

# Divinity in Drag – the Id

Nevertheless, at this point all this accumulated energy that pushes the emergence of the philosophic bands is called *libido*.

## Natural Self Relegated to a Pandora Prison

And as for the pitiful remnant of the Real in the personality — that is, of Mind, of Absolute Subjectivity, of archetypal pattern, of karmic direction and dharmic purposiveness, and of heartfelt human feeling . . . well, that is relegated to a locked and dirty Pandora's box called id — a shabby and distorted remnant, divinity dressed in demonic drag clothing.

And so these years of later childhood continue until the time at which culture and society, the Other, make another significant departure from the reality of self, requiring another radical adaptation. This latest and final duality, this fourth separation, splitting, and shutdown is what I call the fourth fall from grace; and it occurs around the time of puberty.

# SECTION EIGHT

# THE FOURTH FALL FROM GRACE — RITES OF PASSAGE … BECOMING "ADULT"

# 42

# Resistance Is Futile: One Doesn't Have One's Own Mind ... One Takes Up the "Mind" of the "Collective"

*Whence Kitty-Drowners and Butterfly-Mashers: How We Lose Our Selves at Adolescence and Why Conformers and Conservatives in Every Society Hate and Suppress the Rebellious*

## Resistance Is Futile — The Fourth Fall From Grace

Wilber (1977) relates the fourth duality to the rise of the philosophic bands: "In many cases the philosophic bands are instrumental in the generation of the quaternary dualism-repression-projection, and in all cases they are instrumental in its maintenance" (p. 150). Concerning these bands, he quotes Erich Fromm (1970):

*In addition to the social taboos there are individual elaborations of these taboos which differ from family to family; a child, afraid of being "abandoned" by his parents because he is aware of experiences which to them individually are taboo, will, in addition to the socially normal repression [of the Biosocial Band], also repress those feelings which are prevented from coming to awareness by the individual aspect of the filter. (Wilber, 1977, p. 150)*

## Rites of Passage, Becoming "Adult"

The end-result of this fear of parental abandonment that pushes the philosophic bands is what Freud calls the resolution of the oedipal conflict. This splitting and consequent repression/projection corresponds to the rites of passage of puberty and adolescence.

## How We Lose Our Souls

At this point, the child no longer identifies with God (pre-conception), with mother (pre-birth), with body (pre- primal scene), or even with *his* or *her* best idea (one's philosophic ideal); but identifies instead with the same-sex parent, the representative of the social order. Thus he or she becomes totally Other: totally separated from his or her *own* mind (pre- puberty rite); from his or her body (pre- primal scene); from his or her destiny, karma, dharma, duty, and purposiveness (pre-birth); and from God (pre-conception).

## Every Parent's "Atman Project"

This pattern — this doomed and illusory "atman project" wherein the parent seeks to immortalize him- or herself and to redeem his or her life — is of course obvious in the situation of the son "following in his father's footsteps" in taking over the family business and in the daughter's emulation of her mother, traditionally, in the role of wife and mother. But there are many subtler versions of this "identification," and it happens even in situations where it seems it most definitely does not.

For example, Keniston's (1968) study of young radicals of the Sixties — the epitome of rebellious youth, you say — were found to be very much in agreement with their parents' values. In fact, their rebellion was essentially in seeking to put into practice and actually live out what they saw as unlived values and philosophies (hence the charge of "hypocrite") in compromised and compromising parents. Note again the theme of living out the unlived dreams of the previous generation — here, even *in spite of* the conscious stance of those youth.

## Little of Self in the Decision of Who to Be

Cross-culturally and traditionally, however, we see this pattern in perhaps its most rudimentary and clearest form. In a great many cultures, the rites of passage into adulthood embrace the function of bestowing upon and initiating the recipient into the social roles and functions *as decided by the tribe and family*. For most, then, there is little of self in the decision of who to be; it is decided outside of oneself. Corresponding with this, in relation to the marital role, in many cultures the choice of spouse is also decided by others.

## One Continues "Their" Dream ... One's Divine Uniqueness Fades

One doesn't have one's own mind. One takes up the "mind" of the parents, and of society. One continues *their* dream, society's dream. One's divine uniqueness fades into insignificance in the pattern of the social consensual reality.

## Self Is Split Again ... Becoming "Borg" ... Serving the Collective

At any rate, the upshot of all this is that at the quaternary dualism, the self is split again. It is required to give up even "its own mind," its own *concept* of itself. Originally one's divinity was given up; then one's deepest transpersonal directives and organismic unitary awareness; then one's biological rhythms, one's sense of flowingness and inner-directed purposiveness; then one's feelings about self and other; and finally one is required even to give up the best possible *ideas* one can have about oneself and one's relationship to and actions in the world. One represses one's own decisions, initiatives, evaluations, and self-images in conformance to other-directed wants and needs, the result of others' unfulfilled ambitions — which are presented to one by one's parents but represent by extension the other-directed wants and needs of the collective, of the prevailing fear-pushed and desire-pulled economic constraints . . . of the socially-constructed reality in general.

## A "Darkness" Develops

Aminah Raheem (1991) describes the result:

*When the soul becomes so covered over by conditioning that it cannot shine through, when personality completely dominates, a "darkness" develops within the person, characterized by mental or emotional dullness, physical deterioration, accidents, depression, or "bad luck." Such a person seems asleep or unconscious while walking around; she has gotten off her own soul path. (p. 31)*

# Kitty-Drowners and Butterfly-Mashers

And what happens to these repressed dreams, aspirations, initiatives, and values is that, as at previous levels, they are repressed, then projected outside of oneself. Thenceforth they are seen in the world as the "Shadow." Unfortunately, to the extent that we disown and fight these potentials in ourselves, we fight and hate them when we see them outside ourselves.

## Every Society's Culture War

This accounts for the fury with which people will attack and seek to suppress certain individuals and groups who may represent, for example, disowned artistic or creative potentials, disowned aliveness and "charisma," disowned sexuality, disowned intellectual or bohemian dreams, simple disowned "feeling" in general, and anything that smacks of an idealism or freedom or *joie de vivre* that needed especially to be slain in the self in order to make the identification with another's dreams.

Creating in this way the kitty-drowners and butterfly-mashers of the world, the quaternary dualism is complete and, with it, a fourth fall from grace.

## Selling One's Soul

At this point, then, there is very little Self left. In discharging the life that remains — so totally other-directed and other-programmed — one may as well have commissioned an android. Thus we have the endpoint of the spectrum's "evolution" — from divinity to machinery, from pure-Bliss-Consciousness to cybernetic control.

# PART 3

# IMPLICATIONS FOR CHILD "DEVELOPMENT," SPIRITUALITY, AND PERSONAL GROWTH — EGO AND HIGHER CONSCIOUSNESS AND CAN IT BE OTHERWISE

# SECTION NINE

# RETURN TO GRACE — CAN IT BE OTHERWISE?

# 43

## Civilization, Culture, and the History of Our Falls from Grace in Nature: Primal Peoples Had a Nobleness We Don't Know

*Yes, We Can Improve the Human Condition ... and We Have: The Necessary Wound ... We Should Make It Better*

## History of Falls from Grace

In three other works of mine — *Planetmates, The Great Reveal* 2014)*; Primal Renaissance* (1993)*;* and the forthcoming, *Prodigal Human* — I delineate what I believe are some of the factors in creating the present state of consciousness as described as being the endpoint of the process of devolution in the last chapter. I trace it back millions of years to bipedal locomotion, an increasing skull size, greater pain in childbirth, increased psychological repression, changes in pelvic size in the female, the forces of natural selection on the length of gestation, comparative prematurity of human newborns, secondary altriciality, increased pain in infancy and birth for humans, increased repression, increased neocortical capacities, the beginnings of culture, and increased skull size again. I also trace this current patriarchal pathology back thousands of years to the "agrarian revolution" and the rejection of the hunter-gatherer lifestyle.

## Civilization, Culture, and the Falls

So obviously I do not believe that this condition was always the case for us. However, it goes back rather far in our line to the beginnings of our hominid existence. And its more extreme form seems only to have come into existence within the last ten-thousand years, and only then for part of the population. It follows also, since I have claimed that it is more characteristic of "civilized" cultures, that I do not believe that its extreme form is as prevalent in "simpler" cultures, specifically, hunter-gatherer ones. And I should mention that even among hunter-gatherers there is quite a bit of variety in the degree of severity of this expulsion from paradise.

The reason for the disparities between cultures, as can be derived from the model I have constructed, has to do with the fact that we *all*, by virtue of being human, are in a separated state relative to the Divine. We have all come into form, to put it bluntly. Beyond that, we all have some amount of trauma from birth. If nothing else, the separation from the mother represents enough trauma for a secondary duality to occur there; but there is almost always much more than that occurring in the womb or around birth to create a further separated, further removed condition.

So by reason of these species-specific factors, all peoples and all cultures attempt to work out their situation "in darkness" as to the real causes of things, oblivious of the motives behind at least some of their actions, and, in sum, liable to error. Hence, any culture, any people is capable of creating cultural and social constructions that increase, or decrease, the amount of repression and fearfulness that already exists as part of the human condition.

## Primal People

Thus, we can only say that *in general* hunter-gatherers are less repressed, less anxious, less "devolved," and so on, than are people from agrarian or industrial cultures. Cultures have taken somewhat different paths, even hunter-gatherer ones (cf. Gregor, 1985; and Turnbull, 1972). But generalities have their uses, and the evidence appears overwhelming that simpler lifestyles are correlated with radically different, more humane attitudes and behaviors toward children, toward other human beings, and toward Nature in general — characterizing a less split-off state. (cf. Bird-David, 1992; French, 1985; Lawlor, 1991; Liedloff, 1977; Sahlins, 1972; Turnbull, 1961; and van der Post, 1986).

# The Necessary Wound?

Also, this analysis does not take into account any metaphysical or theological perspectives on the opportunities or, dare I say, "benefits" of a separated state, a more dismal and painful human condition. There are those who claim that this "wounding" is a necessary prerequisite to truly human compassion and empathy. Muller (1992) has said that the painful and traumatic human condition ... and he is speaking particularly of that produced in childhood ... represents our unique *opportunity* ... he even uses the term *advantage*.

Still, hunter-gatherers do not seem to be any the less compassionate or empathetic; indeed, the opposite of that is most often asserted about them. So one must conclude that there is no reason to go back to the poisonous pedagogical traditions which enjoined that sparing the rod would spoil the child, or to Christian, especially Catholic, ones that routed the roadways to heaven through valleys of torture (to which I can personally attest).

## We Should Make It Better

It would seem, to the extent we are able, that we should do all in our power to minimize this devolutional pull on consciousness, to do all in our power to minimize the separation from the source of our true identity, our knowing, our power and joy; to do all in our power to maximize the chances for future generations, as well as ourselves, to live in the nobleness, strength, at-home-ness, and glow of divinity that characterizes our species at its best. I am sure, given that, that there would still be enough "darkness" hereabouts — within our still-separated state — to go around, providing more than enough "opportunities" and "advantages" for any other ends God might have in mind for us.

## Can We Make It Better?

So, then, the question still remaining is, can it be otherwise? Can we make it better? Can we improve the human condition? Looking cross-culturally, the answer would appear to be absolutely in the affirmative (Lyn-Piluso & Lyn-Piluso, 1994). From the perspective of the new experiential psychotherapies, ditto. From the viewpoint of conscious and responsible conception (Baker, 1986) and loving and welcoming gestation (Verny, 1981), without a doubt. And from that of humane and natural birthing procedures (Leboyer, 1975); sensitive, physical, and loving infant care (Liedloff, 1977); and flexible, attentive, and accepting child care-giving (Mahler et al, 1975; Sroufe et al, 1992); a resounding yes!

So let us look now at some of the evidence for a more fortunate and favorable human condition and some of the factors correlated with it. With those in mind, we can envision the more natural self.

# 44

# Changing the Human Condition Starts with Birth: The Most Precocious, Brilliant, and Advanced Children Were Treated Differently as Newborns

*Building the Better Human ... We Do Not Need to*
*Traumatize Our Babies: Doing Better About Birth*

## So Much About Smiling

We can start with the example of "social smiling." Mainstream psychology and child development claim that "social smiling" does not occur in the infant until about four or five months, that even "true" *pleasure* smiling does not develop until around ten weeks, attributing any smiling that occurs before that either to "spontaneous discharge in lower brain regions" or "to gas." (Sroufe et al, 1992, especially pp. 196-201).

Yet, Leboyer (1975) reported that babies who had entered the world in the humane manner of delivery he developed smile frequently and often from the day of birth. These babies also show physical and emotional advantages way above average. At any rate, it is hard to believe that newborns with the physical and emotional advantages of such a loving and beautiful welcome as is described and attested to for Leboyer babies are having all that much more gas than babies given the normal, harsh hospital welcome.

## Our Arrogant Inability to Impute Consciousness to Beings Other Than Us

In addition, the research used to support this idea that infant smiling is not indicative of pleasure has to do with the fact that this smiling occurs regularly for the infant upon going to sleep and that "If their smiles are a sign of pleasure, why don't they occur when infants are wide awake as well?" (Sroufe et al, 1992, p. 197).

This statement is laughable considering only what I have said so far. For we know that babies *do* smile when awake, in fact a lot of the time, specifically, Leboyer babies. But beyond that, the reasoning involved in it clearly displays some of the problems with the Newtonian-Cartesian paradigm I mentioned previously. It seems we find it extremely hard to impute consciousness and awareness to beings other than ourselves . . . and that the furthest from our normal state another conscious state is, the more likely we are to deny its existence.

## Feeling That We Have Been Forced to Give Up Our Awareness, We Want to Deny Awareness in Others

The reasons for this refusal to acknowledge awareness should be apparent from the devolutional model, where we see, for example, that with each additional splitting of consciousness, at each, so called, "stage of development," the individual is further reduced in awareness until, as Huxley (1954) put it, "all that remains is the measly trickle of awareness necessary for survival on this planet." So it makes sense, feeling that we have been forced to give up our awareness, we will want to deny awareness to others. And, of course, we can get away with this all the more with those most unlike us, where we can expect community support in this kind of mutual illusory neurosis and scapegoating.

But keep in mind that we are attempting here to maintain the new-paradigm insistence on the prior reality of consciousness. So let us not stray from that and let us see just what is implied by this statement from the mainstream that babies do not feel pleasure because it happens regularly when they are falling off to sleep. To put it bluntly, if I smile every time I have an orgasm, with strict conformity to certain specific neurophysiological characteristics each and every time, does that mean my orgasms are not pleasurable?

## Don't We Have a Say in How We Feel?

Well, if I were a mainstream psychologist I might have to say, yes, it means that they are not pleasurable. Looking at me from the outside, and not including the factor of my subjectivity — which would cause them to ask *me* whether or not it was pleasure, to grant me that much respect — they would have to conclude in the negative. However, I would have to disagree with them. And I feel the newborn would probably disagree with them also, if she or he could but speak.

Since he or she cannot, I submit that we should at least leave the question open, rather, that we should assume it is not all that much different from our own experience of smiling and pleasure rather than to err in the direction of concocting bizarre explanations whose main benefit can only be to prop up crumbling and outdated paradigms.

# Building the Better Human — Birth and Infancy

But to continue, on this same issue of smiling, we get support cross-culturally that the human condition, as I have described it above, mostly for Westerners, can be different. Pearce (1980) writes concerning the supposed lack of intelligence and lack of social smiling in the Western newborn:

*No less than Jerome Bruner of Harvard's Center for Cognitive Studies, surely one of our more brilliant researchers developed this idea. The assumption is terribly wrong, but the academic rationale growing around it began to include more contradictions blithely ignored because once an idea is accepted into the body of knowledge, everyone "knows" and no one questions it. Everyone "knew" that no smiling occurs for some ten to twelve weeks because infants are born prematurely and have no intelligence during that time. If a mother reported smiling before that acceptable date, the cryptic diagnosis was "gas pains." (p. 42)*

Can it be otherwise? Looking cross-culturally, it appears to be so. Pearce (1980) writes further,

*In 1956, Marcelle Geber . . . made a momentous discovery. She found the most precocious, brilliant, and advanced infants and children observed anywhere. These infants had smiled, continuously and rapturously, from, at the latest, their fourth day of life. Blood analyses showed that all the adrenal steroids connected with birth stress were totally absent by that fourth day after birth. Sensorimotor learning and general development were phenomenal, indeed miraculous. These Ugandan infants were months ahead of American or European children. A superior intellectual development held for the first four years of life. . .*

.

*These infants were born in the home, generally delivered by the mother herself. The child was never separated from the mother, who massaged, caressed, sang to, and fondled her infant continually. She slept with her infant. The infant fed continuously, according to its own schedule. These infants were awake a surprising amount of time — alert, watchful, happy, calm. They virtually never cried. Their mothers were bonded to them . . . and sensed their every need before that need had to be expressed by crying. The mother responded to the infant's every gesture and assisted the child in any and every move that was undertaken, so that every move initiated by the child ended in immediate success. At two days of age (forty-eight hours) these infants sat bolt upright, held only by the forearms, with a beautifully straight back and perfect head balance, their finely focused eyes staring intently, intelligently at their mothers. And they smiled and smiled. (pp. 42-43)*

# 45

## The Primal Scene and the Divine Child: Hierarchical Societies Demand Conformity All the Way Down the Line

*Becoming "as a Child" and Building the Better Human —*
*Childhood: The Ego Is Sycophantic to Someone and "The*
*Word" — What Those Voices You Hear Really Are*

Let us turn now to the third fall from grace, that time when the child's potential is reduced to the acceptable spectrum, only, that reflects the socionormative constructs of the society. Can this be different?

## Primal Scene — We Give Up

Remember that at the primal scene, occurring around the age of four or five, we become "them." We give up. We see our attempts to interact as ourselves with our parents and the world extending out from them as being utterly futile. We feel it is better to get at least something by being someone they want rather to get nothing and to seethe in loneliness and inattention being the unique person we were meant to be.

## The Unreal Self, the Ego, Is Sycophantic to Someone

So, we cater to others' requirements and lose connection with our own wants and needs ... *their* needs become our needs.

We develop an unreal self which is concocted to please others and comprised of bargaining chips to procure approval from others. Our self is sycophantic to someone. Even if that self contains elements of "toughness" or independence, those traits came into being to placate another, usually the same-sex parent.

## "Child Sacrifice"

I say it is comparable to "child sacrifice" and is exemplified in Western culture in the Biblical story of Abraham being told by "God" to sacrifice his son, Isaac. For "God," you may read the insane workings of the mind in adult life once one has lost a real and felt connection to the transpersonal by means of these falls from grace. You see here, over and again, that we do to others what has been done to us. Having been forced to give up ourselves we are *compelled* ... by "God," but actually by the end products of emotional pain ... to slay that same thing in our children when it presents itself.

I say it is the fall from grace that occurs as a result of relationship trauma. Indeed, it is that which develops at the time when the child is beginning to connect with the wider world beyond Mother. The earlier traumas and splittings from innate divinity come about in relation to the mother or other primary care-giver. They happen at and around birth and for a while afterward through the interaction of the infant with mother around gestation, actual birth, and then, bonding, nursing, feeding, toilet training, and so on.

While this pressure to split off from the body and its needs and the transpersonal and its directives and guidance continues into toddlerhood, more and more the child interacts with siblings, other children, the father, the other figures in the social unit.

So, as with the mother, the natural child will seek to have its needs satisfied. Earlier this was for biological needs. Now this is for relational needs ... connection with others, interaction, mutual recognition. So over time the biological and affectional needs develop and become related to ways of behaving and interacting around needs of belongingness and connection with loved ones in the immediate family. Ideally these needs are met through mutual recognition and appreciation between distinct human personalities.

# Hierarchical Societies Demand Conformity All the Way Down the Line

However, in complex, hierarchical societies and just like in the Abraham and Isaac myth, the parents will seek to have their children behave and appear to be like miniature versions of themselves ... mini-me's. Like Abraham, the adult is not really seeing the child and its needs as separate from his or her own. Rather the parent is caught up in the mental byproducts of unmet needs from his or her own childhood. Indeed, the child becomes a byproduct of the adult's attempt to orchestrate the emotional pain within him or herself.

### "The Word": Those Voices You Hear ... What They Really Are

How that manifests is that the adult — all the while proclaiming to be doing this "for the child's own good" — will seek to carve a reflection of him or herself into the precious sensitivity of the toddler and preschooler.

Without a doubt, the adult thinks it is doing this in obedience to voices coming from outside. For they are the pushes and pulls of his or her own unmet needs in childhood, which — repressed because of the pain associated with them and existing in a portion of the consciousness ... and brain ... not accessible to consciousness — now have influence seemingly from the outside.

The fact that the adult will feel that these unconscious forces have the force of a higher power ... a deity in Abraham's case ... is because they indeed are the remnants of instructions, nonverbal messages, and admonitions given to that adult as a child from his or her own parents. Coming from outside oneself they seem to come from a supernatural source. Coming from one's parents they seem to come from a higher source ... one requiring strict obedience ... one's parents.

## The "Commandments" and the Culture's Shared Neurosis

Beyond that, they appear to come from a higher authority since these "commandments" from the parents are reflective of the society as a whole. For the cookie cutter that is pressed upon the precocious personality of the young one and which is in the shape of the parent is somewhat like the cookie cutters of that culture in general. That is to say, the neurotic proclivities of an adult in any society are of course going to be similar to those of the others in that society, for indeed neurosis is all about conformity with others. Put bluntly, the way the parent's soul has been disfigured is roughly in the manner of the way others in that society have been disfigured.

## "Doctrine" of Infallibility

So, being reflective of the larger society, again the patterns of this unreal self have that sense of being from "above" — from outside oneself and from higher up. Thus, these distorted orchestrations on the self from the outside carry with them all the weight and validity as from an infallible source ... though of course that is anything but true.

I should at least mention at this point that the reason this process of losing one's self in conformity to supposedly higher others is more extreme in complex, "civilized," societies is because the hierarchical nature of such societies imposes itself upon all elements of its corresponding culture. Specifically, in such societies virtually all adults are pressured into conformity with higher ups of some sort or other and are sycophantic in relation to them. Naturally this pattern of oppression in the greater society will be reflected in the patterns of relationship in the family as well.

# Building the Better Human — Childhood

## A Child Wants to Be of Service by Nature

Now, by contrast to Western attitudes to young children, Liedloff (1977) describes the kind of trust in the innate sociality of the child and the "respect" for the child and for his or her "inclinations" that characterized the Yequana:

*Perhaps as essential as the assumption of innate sociality in children and adults is a respect for each individual as his own proprietor. The notion of ownership of other persons is absent among the Yequana. The idea that this is "my child" or "your child" does not exist. Deciding what another person should do, no matter what his age, is outside the Yequana vocabulary of behaviors. There is great interest in what everyone does, but no impulse to influence — let alone coerce — anyone. A child's will is his motive force. There is no slavery — for how else can one describe imposing one's will on another and coercion by threat and punishment? The Yequana do not feel that a child's inferior physical strength and dependence upon them imply that they should treat him or her with less respect than an adult. No orders are given a child that run counter to his own inclinations as to how to play, how much to eat, when to sleep, and so on.*

*But where his help is required, he is expected to comply instantly. Commands like "Bring some water!" "Chop some wood!" "Hand me that!" or "Give the baby a banana!" are given with the same assumption of innate sociality, in the firm knowledge that a child wants to be of*

*service and to join in the work of his people. No one watches to see
whether the child obeys — there is no doubt of his will to cooperate. As
the social animal he is, he does as he is expected without hesitation and
to the very best of his ability. (pp. 90-91)*

## An Example of the Adult Role Containing Within It Also the Real Self, the Child

In a similar fashion, the Mbuti, as described by Turnbull (1961), hardly notice a difference from child roles and expectations and adult ones:

*And one day they find that the games they have been playing are not
games any longer, but the real thing, for they have become adults. Their
hunting is now real hunting; their tree climbing is in earnest search of
inaccessible honey; their acrobatics on the swings are repeated almost
daily, in other forms, in the pursuit of elusive game, or in avoiding the
malicious forest buffalo. It happens so gradually that they hardly notice
the change at first, for even when they are proud and famous hunters
their life is still full of fun and laughter. (p. 129)*

## The Divine Child

The holy man from India, Sathya Sai Baba, echoes these perspectives of the child as presented by Pearce (1980) and demonstrated in nonliterate cultures. He says, "The human child sees itself as the center of the universe and the world as an extension of its being. This divine child knows that it is so" (1991, p. 295).

Kasturi (1991), Baba's editor and translator explains,

*Children are most concerned with the Now; Baba reminds us the past is
past; do not turn back and look wistfully or wailingly on the road you
have traversed already. Children do not see the world as fragmented by
walls: Chinese, Berlinese, or erected just to tease; they are involved in*

*everything and with everyone; they represent true innocence, love, forgiveness and fraternity. The child has no conceit or contempt of gender; this divine child [referring to the avatar, Sai Baba] affirms: "Among men I am man; among women I am woman; among children I am a child." (p. 295)*

*This child [meaning Sathya Sai Baba] inspires us to become children again so that we might be ever with Him, of Him, in Him. (p. 295)*

# 46

# By Adolescence "Civilized" Children Are Programmed ... Whereas in Primal Societies Inner Experience Is Cultivated: Puberty, Becoming Adult

*"Civilization" Brings Brutal Rites of Passage and Fear of the Supernatural: The People of Nature Just Laugh at the Townsfolk Living in Such Terror and Valuing Cruelty*

Finally, let us investigate the fourth fall from grace, the time around puberty when the ego is consolidated around a specific identity, task, role that marks her or him for life. Can this be otherwise?

## Forest and Village Worldviews Are Directly at Odds

Once again, Turnbull's (1961) report on the Mbuti provides a fitting example. This example is especially illuminating in that he was able to observe and note differences between the hunter-gatherer Mbuti and nearby villagers with whom they had occasional contact. Since the villagers have to be considered post-agrarian and definitely not hunter-gatherers, we are able to study any differences between these two lifestyles and possible differences in worldview, side-by-side.

## With "Civilization" Comes Brutal Rites of Adulthood and Excessive "Masculinity"

Indeed, Turnbull shows that these differences do exist, and we see one distinctly in connection to the rites of passage that are undergone respectively in each culture.

The rite of passage is called the *nkumbi* and is conducted by the villagers. The Pygmies undergo it, at a certain age, in order to enjoy certain respect and privileges in their dealings with villagers, as they must often have for various reasons. Of their own, the Mbuti have no such rite of passage, certainly nothing severe and harsh like that of the villagers. Turnbull (1961) describes the villagers' *nkumbi*:

*The physical ordeals sometimes start out as games but develop into cruel tests of physical endurance. A crouching dance that might be fun for a few minutes becomes agony after half an hour. A mild switching on the underside of the arm with light sticks is of no concern until, after several days, the skin becomes raw. And then the villagers notch the sticks so that they fold over and pinch the skin sharply, often drawing blood. When the boys have become used to being beaten with leafy branches, thorny bushes are substituted. (p. 225)*

## Dominant Societies Try to Instill Fear of the Supernatural to Control Their Underlings

He also explains the villagers beliefs concerning this rite of passage and its effect and purpose:

*The villagers believed that the initiate, Pygmy or otherwise, is everlastingly bound thereafter by all the laws of the tribe, sacred and secular. He is put into direct relationship with the supernatural, whose representatives on earth are the villagers themselves. If any Pygmy initiate offends a villager, therefore, he is also offending the supernatural — the ancestors — and will be duly punished by them. The villagers live in such fear of the supernatural, with its power to bring down on an offender the curses of leprosy, yaws, dysentery and other diseases or to cause him to be injured by a falling tree, that they cannot conceive of any initiates daring to offend the ancestors. (p. 224)*

## But Primal Folks Laugh at the Fears of "Domesticated" Humans and Delight in Flaunting Their Customs

But offend the ancestors they do, these Pygmies, and with apparent relish. They do not share the villagers fearful view of the world. They cannot imagine any good reason to inflict these tortures on each other and laugh, secretly, behind the villagers' backs, at them. Turnbull (1961) writes,

*Both the boys and their fathers enjoyed the chance to make fun, in a friendly way, of the villagers, but that was not their sole reason for deliberately breaking all the taboos. They behaved as they did because to them the restrictions were not only meaningless but belonged to a hostile world. The villagers hoped that the nkumbi would place the Pygmies directly under the supernatural authority of the village tribal ancestors; the Pygmies naturally took good care that nothing of the sort should happen, proving it to themselves by this conscious flaunting of custom. (p. 224)*

# Building the Better Human – Entry Into Adulthood

*To the Pygmies this all seems harsh and unnecessary, and as far as their own children are concerned they keep a strict watch over them to see*

231

*that the villagers do not go to the length that they sometimes do with village children, even if this brings them into some contempt. But to the villager this toughening-up process is essential and does not come naturally in the course of village life. The child has to be fitted for adult life, and this is what the nkumbi sets out to achieve. In a few months a boy becomes a man, tough and strong, physically and mentally. The process is not a pleasant one, but it is the only way in which, under tribal conditions, the goal can be achieved.*

*The Pygmy can understand and appreciate this, but the very nature of his own nomadic hunting and gathering existence provides all the toughening up and education that are needed. Children begin climbing trees sometimes before they can walk. Their muscles develop, and they overcome fear in a number of daring tree games. Adult activities are learned from an early age by observation and imitation, for the Pygmies live an open life.*

*Their life is as open inside their tiny one-room leaf huts as it is in the middle of a forest clearing, and so the children have no need of the sex instruction which forms so large a part of the teaching given to village boys during the nkumbi. (pp. 225-226)*

*Far from illustrating the dependence of the Pygmies upon the villagers, the nkumbi illustrates better than anything else the complete opposition of the forest to the village. The Pygmies in the forest consciously and energetically reject all village values. When they are in the village they temporarily adopt its values and customs, not wanting to desecrate their sacred forest values by bringing them into the village. That is why they never sing their sacred songs in the village the way they do in the forest, and why they refuse to consecrate the nkumbi with special music, although every other event of importance in their lives is marked in this way. There is an unbridgeable gulf between the two worlds of the two peoples.*

*The Pygmies have their own way of growing naturally into adulthood. A boy proves himself capable of supporting a family when he kills his first real game, and proves himself a man when he participates in the elima. (p. 227)*

## By Adolescence in "Civilized" Societies Most Children Have Had the "Still Small Voice" Programmed Out, Whereas in Primal Cultures It is Valued

Aminah Raheem (1991) gives a final example of how this stage can be different in other cultures:

*By the onset of adolescence, most children are intricately programmed into the cultural complex of their time and place. The "still small voice" of the soul is rarely heard and, when it is, it is usually discarded as fantasy or nonsense. For example, when I worked with late adolescents, I found that they often received deep soul promptings through dreams of visionary experiences. These numinous events seemed to contain valuable guidance for direction in their lives, but usually they were discounted by the dreamers and their peers as fantasy. By contrast, in American Indian culture such experiences are valued as clear messages of life purpose, especially when they appear during puberty. (p. 29)*

# 47

# What Does the Natural Self Look Like? The State of Not Losing the Soul Is Emotional Openness and Joy, Being Equally Free in Tears and Laughter

*Integrated with The Way, One Becomes "Lighter" Through Life ... Expansive Soul Energy Dances Through the Person: The Natural Self*

## Return to Grace

What can be the result of making these kinds of changes? Once again I look cross-culturally to give examples. But looking at the extraordinary childhoods of particular people provides contrast and insight also.

### The Natural Self

First, let us hear how Turnbull (1961) describes the results of the more trusting, more respectful childhood of the Mbuti.[1] He describes the emotional openness and joy that characterizes the Pygmy adult:

*When Pygmies laugh it is hard not to be affected; they hold onto one another as if for support, slap their sides, snap their fingers, and go through all manner of physical contortions. If something strikes them as particularly funny they will even roll on the ground. . . . (p. 44)*

*They clapped one another on the back and held onto one another for support as they laughed, inventing all sorts of things they would do and say to any girl who answered them in such a way. The Pygmy is not in the least self-conscious about showing his emotions; he likes to laugh until tears come to his eyes and he is too weak to stand. He then sits down or lies on the ground and laughs still louder. (p. 56)*

## Equally Open to Grief and to Laughter

But this is not to mean that they do not feel sorrow. In fact, quite the opposite is the case. They seem to be equally as open to grief as to laughter, able to go into either deeply and fully. Considering all we are being taught by counseling psychologists on the need to fully have a period of grief when confronted by loss, it may be that we need to look to the Pygmy temperament as an example of that ideal. Turnbull (1961) relates,

*But when someone really dies, for ever, there is among the Pygmies a burst of uncontrollable grief, not only from the relatives, but from friends. Even men will weep if they have been close to the dead person. It is a very different sound, and a terrible one. . . . (p. 42)*

# The Way

Raheem (1991) describes her understanding of the state of not losing the soul, which apparently happens in some unusual people.

*On the other hand, the person who follows her own soul and uses the*

*vehicle of personality to execute its purpose, will become "lighter" through life. There will be a sense of flowing easily from one moment to the next, as though she were in a beautifully choreographed dance which she had thoroughly mastered.*

*The free, expansive soul energy can dance through the whole person, bringing creativity, spontaneity and vitality throughout mind, body and emotions. And since such a person is on course, integrated with her own Tao, she can experience strength, tranquility and certainty from within herself. (p. 31)*

SECTION TEN

# CORRECTING THE "CIVILIZED" EGO — THE STORMY PATH TO SELF

# 48

# Is the Supernatural Terrifying? The Idea of a Shamanistic, Stormy Spiritual Path Is Too at Odds with Our Religious Anti-Body Culture to Be Easily Accepted

*Correcting the "Civilized" Ego ... The Way Forward Is Down: The Divine Is Mistaken for "the Devil" Until One Is Surrendered Enough*

## Implications of Falls from Grace, The Devolutional Model of Development

From looking at the possibility of a more benign, less tragic human trajectory, as we did in the last section, I would now like to delve into the implications of this devolutional model of development — these Falls from Grace — as concerns psychotherapy, human growth, or "healing." For, once the falls have happened to a person, once the patriarchal pathology has occurred, we need to look at what to do about it. We need to turn from prevention, as in the previous section, to correction or remediation.

## The Way Forward Is Down

I said at the outset of Part 2 that a metaphorical analysis such as this one can uncover underlying meanings: It can provide understanding of inner and outer behavior as well as guidance for such. At this point it can be stated that the implications of an analysis such as I have been presenting are for no less than the direction of growth, the direction of mystical experience, the concept of regression, and the evaluation of current ego psychotherapies, among others.

## Is a "Fully Functioning Ego" a Prerequisite to Higher Consciousness?

Specifically, this perspective puts in question the psychotherapeutic maxim that ego strength precedes higher consciousness. I confess that many years ago I myself made exactly that claim in a work titled *The Dangers of Mysticism for Modern Youth* (Adzema, 1970). As I concluded, "Cosmic consciousness is dependent upon self-actualization." By this I meant, following a Jungian line, that ego-actualization leading to a solidified ego and ego strength was necessary before one could hope to face the overwhelming and terrifying Unconscious Self — the repressed inner Divinity. And again following Jung, I proposed that this usually could not occur until the second half of life, or after the mid-life crisis.

## Is the Supernatural Terrifying?

Subsequently, however, I encountered the new experiential psychotherapeutic techniques which — it has been my own experience — allow one to deal with and integrate the repressed "negative" energies that lie along the path (as this book's analysis demonstrates) to mystical experience of Energy, Mind, Absolute Subjectivity, and God. Thus, although I was offered an opportunity to do so in an esteemed professional journal, I could not in good conscience publish that earlier work.

## Ego Does Not Precede Illumination, It Prohibits It

Schneider (1987), to give an example, claims that the kind of mystical consciousness of which Wilber speaks is not possible because, for one thing, it would be terrifying and overwhelming.

Indeed, that was a good part of my position in *The Dangers of Mysticism for Modern Youth* (Adzema, 1970). But as I say, I eventually came to understand there to be a big difference between *access to* and *integration of* these realities. For, as both Jung and Campbell have pointed out, a God is often seen as a devil until one is wholly enough ... I would say surrendered enough ... to approach him.

## Some People Are Sick for Healthy Reasons

At any rate, those subsequent experiences of mine with the experiential psychotherapies led to a reformulation of my understanding which led to works titled, descriptively enough, "The Way Forward Is Down" (1972a) and *The Centered Path Through Hell* (1972b). The proposition arising from this later work is that *low* self-esteem, *low* ego strength, is a precondition for "higher" ("lower") growth in a mystical direction.

As Maslow (1968) put it (and contrary to Wilber [1970]), some people are sick for sick reasons and some people are sick for healthy reasons. Therefore, especially in an avowed "insane" (see Fromm, 1955) culture, we might want to think twice about doing people the big favor of "helping" them in the direction of increased ego defenses ... and societal adjustment and social functioning.

In fact, those people with inadequate defenses against what is in essence more real are not only closer to being *truly* sane than the majority of folks but also might be better helped by leading them in the direction of dismantling what remains of the barriers between themselves and pure Energy, pure Consciousness, and helping them instead to integrate with and grow to encompass the expanded awareness that results.

# The Stormy Path to Self

Now, I realize that this proposition is not absolutely new. For one thing it seems to make sense of some of the extreme and bizarre behavior, the seemingly manifest neurotic behavior, of some of the saints and mystics on their way to expanded awareness (see for example James, 1899/1982, especially Henry Suso, pp. 306-310; and Saint John of the Cross, 1959).

But in this secular age, it seems such allowance for "aberrant" behavior is rare. Keep in mind that in many cultures there are institutions — like medieval monasteries — or roles, like shamans, through and in which such distortions of personality can be worked out in socially sanctioned ways. Contrast this with the modern attitude which seems to be that if they cannot be talked into picking themselves up and/or behaving themselves like everyone else they are to be drugged or electroshocked into compliance.

Nevertheless, there are those in this day also who do speak out in favor of the direction of growth that this book is presenting. R. D. Laing, Arthur Janov, and Stanislav Grof are not the least of these. Indeed, Stanislav and Christina Grof's (1990) book, *The Stormy Search for the Self*, is a near-exact affirmation of the proposition I have just stated.

## Our Religious, Anti-Body Culture Makes Folks Terrified of the Shamanistic, Stormy Path

Still, this idea of a "stormy" spiritual path — despite the fact that it was distinctively presented and described over a century ago in William James's classic work, *The Varieties of Religious Experience*, (1899/1982) — in my opinion, goes too much against our hard won "rationality" … which we see is essentially our cultural *rationalization*. This notion is too much an affront to our culturally embedded "pragmatism" … which it is clear now is our cop-out to consensual constructs, especially fear-rooted economic ones. And it is in direct opposition to our pervasive Judeo-Christian anti-body cultural bias. So this idea of a stormy spiritual path, a path in which progress involves regress … in which the way forward is down, is anything but easily accepted.

# 49

# "Crazy" and Transcendent Are Not Opposite as Ego Psychologists Conveniently Proclaim: Have Western Puritanical Beliefs Infected Transpersonal Psychology?

*The Linear Fallacy and Ken Wilber's Fall from Grace:*
*Spiritual Growth Is Hardly Linear ... You Can't Put*
*"Enlightenment" on Your To-Do List*

## The Linear Fallacy

### Cybernetic Dreaming

Even in the field of transpersonal psychology, for example, there seems an inability to accept such a visceral, energetic, cathartic, "Dionysian," spiritual path — a "surrendered" one ... a shamanistic one. Instead we see a tendency to opt for "Apollonian" head trips, mere relaxation and visualizations, cybernetic ego programming and affirmations, and rational-intellectual metaphoristics — a "controlling" path (cf., Berman, 1986, "Cybernetic Dream").

We hear that one must have an ego before one can lose one ... as if we all, from birth, don't have *some* kind of ego! We hear that there are "healthy" ego defenses to have ... as if all defenses are not in some way the avoidance or distortion of truth.

## Ken Wilber's Mistake

Interestingly, Ken Wilber — who, along with Stanislav Grof, is considered a fountainhead of modern transpersonal psychology — has been, at different times, on both sides of this development. His change of position from *The Spectrum of Consciousness* (1977) to *The Atman Project* (1980) is, in my opinion, regrettable. Obviously, from the analysis presented in this book, *Falls from Grace*, it is clear that I believe that his stance at the outset, in *The Spectrum of Consciousness*, is closer to the truth.

## The Prepersonal and the Transpersonal Are Not Separate

Further, I agree with Washburn (1990) that Wilber's espousal of a prepersonal/transpersonal distinction (Wilber, 1982) — which predicates his change of position — "assumes a major point at issue," specifically, that "'pre' and 'trans' states are totally unrelated, and are in fact opposites," and that Wilber does not establish this position empirically (p. 94). Similarly, while I regret the use to which Schneider (1987) puts this information, I concur with him that "a careful reading of the case evidence does not — as Wilber . . . would have it — clearly differentiate (prepersonal) psychotics from truly (transpersonal) visionaries" (p. 202).

## Ken Wilber's Pre/Trans Distinction — Does Not Fit with the Evidence

In sum, the operative factor in Wilber's change of position, which is also a basic building block of all of his later theory — that is to say, the pre/trans distinction — does not fit with the evidence from the spiritual or psychiatric literatures. It certainly does not fit with the evidence of experiential psychotherapy and pre- and perinatal psychology. Finally, as Epstein and Leiff (1981, p. 140) pointed out, neither does his hypothesis appear to fit with the evidence of meditation research.

## One Returns to the Beginning, Again and Again

As Grof (1985) said concerning Wilber's pre/trans distinction:

*My own observations suggest that, as consciousness evolution proceeds from the centauric to the subtle realms and beyond, it does not follow a linear trajectory, but in a sense enfolds into itself.*

*In this process, the individual returns to earlier stages of development, but evaluates them from the point of view of a mature adult. At the same time, he or she becomes consciously aware of certain aspects and qualities of these stages that were implicit, but unrecognized when confronted in the context of linear evolution.*

*Thus, the distinction between pre- and trans- has a paradoxical nature; they are neither identical, nor are they completely different from each other. (p. 137)*

# Ken Wilber's Fall from Grace

Indeed why Wilber, while acknowledging Grof at least, would choose not to incorporate the findings of prenatal and perinatal psychology and would opt instead for a Piaget-based theory of development that begins (1) at birth (1980, p. 6) and (2) with the self identified with matter that is defined as lowest consciousness (1980, p. $x$ and p. 7) — a Piaget-based theory that is radically altered by prenatal and perinatal psychology and consciousness research in general (see Grof; Pearce, 1980) — is a mystery in itself.

## The Alpha and the Omega Meet

By that I mean that (1) Wilber ignores the first nine months of an individual's life, as if those experiences — which others, and myself in this book, have shown to be all-important — are not only not influential but non-existent!

By that I also mean that (2) Wilber (1980) claims that at birth the self is identified with matter (p. *x* and p. 7), which he calls the *pleroma* and which he states is a gnostic term for the *virgo mater* or *materia prima* (p. 20). First of all, my reading of gnosticism does not tell me that the pleroma is a primal matter but rather a primal *spiritual* source from which all else — specifically, matter — *devolves*.

Gnostic writings tell that, in fact, the creation of matter and the world occurs later, much later in the course of devolution than the "spiritual" pleroma. They tell also that the material universe comes in only with the creation of the inferior god, the Demiurge (the ego); and that it is a *flawed* creation — one might say it is one that no longer adequately reflects spirit and that it has fallen from grace. (See Robinson, 1988, *The Nag Hammadi Library in English*)

## "God Is All There Is."

This may seem a minor point; however, its implications are huge for Wilber's theory and it indicates exactly where we differ. What I am saying is that, from a particular perspective — one might say a *gnostic* one — matter is from spirit (or Consciousness), is of the same stuff as spirit (except that it is flawed). That really and truly what we see "out there" is spirit and is no different from what we experience "in here" save that our sensory experience is an imperfect — one might say, reflected or indirect — experience . . . but of the same thing! *This* is indeed the implication of the new physics and the new psychology. As one song, a bhajan, sums it up: "God is all. God is all there is." (See, also, Adzema, 2013, *Experience Is Divinity.*)

Now, Wilber knew this in *The Spectrum of Consciousness*; he espoused this perspective in that book. That he later turned from this radical spiritual perspective on matter; this mystical, Eastern, "new physics," psychedelic, and Platonic perspective on the material world and sensory experience . . . well, one might say he "fell from grace."

## The Stormy Path to Self

As Grof (1985) has exclaimed concerning Wilber:

*It is . . . somewhat surprising that he has not taken into consideration a vast amount of data from both ancient and modern sources — data suggesting the paramount psychological significance of prenatal experiences and the trauma of birth. (pp. 135-136)*

Further, concerning Wilber's theoretical system:

*The complexity of embryonic development and of the consecutive stages of biological birth receives no attention in this sophisticated system, which is elaborated in meticulous detail in all other areas. (p. 136)*

## You Can't "Program" Your Way Into Transcendence

It seems that Wilber (1980, 1982), however — as one of the chief proponents of the ego-quest-as-precondition-to-spiritual-quest school of transpersonal thought — has made the mistake of constructing his transpersonal argument within the gravitational field of the Western ego psychologists. Thus it ends up helplessly skewed in that direction. He completely ignores the evidence cross-culturally for the ego weakness that most often characterizes mystical adherents and religious practitioners.

## Ken Wilber's Cop-Out

Hence, Wilber's overall position is muddied in contradiction. See, for example, *A Sociable God.* Here Wilber says adolescence includes previous structures:

*As the adolescent mind emerges, it destroys the exclusive identity with the body but does not destroy the body itself; it subsumes the body in its own larger mental identity. (1983, p. 104)*

Now, compare that with *The Spectrum of Consciousness*(1977) in which he contends that each stage splits off from and *represses* previously "owned" realities making them unconscious.

There are no two ways to interpret this: In the earlier work, he saw a reduction, or devolution, in consciousness with each subsequent stage in consciousness — exactly the position I espouse in this book. Whereas by the latter work, *A Sociable God,* he himself has become more conforming with societal beliefs, more "sociable," and becomes an apologist for the status quo. He begins rationalizing — as people tend to do as they get older and more split off from their real feelings — that it was not "all that" repressed after all when one went from one stage to the other of the spectrum.

This is the transpersonal psychology equivalent of the older person, tired of the emotional baggage carried from a traumatic childhood, resigning herself to saying that, well, Daddy (or Mommy) actually did love her "in his *own* way." The point is this is not about truth anymore. It is about giving up the struggle for truth and conforming to whatever beliefs make life easier ... or in Wilber's case, facilitate one on the career "ladder."

## Transcendent States Require Pre-Egoic Integration

At any rate, I think the integration of Wilber's work with that of Grof, primal psychology, Masters and Houston, and the new prenatal and perinatal information from various sources helps to clarify some of the confusion resulting from his change of position.[1]

My hope also is that my work in this book in integrating all of the above, including Wilber's schema, goes at least some part of the way toward correcting the misunderstanding that arises from his omissions.

# 50

# Ego Weak Mystics and Shamans: A Supremely Defended Ego Is the Aim of Modern "Sanitized" Spirituality ... the "Holy Fools" of Mystical History Would Be Medicated Today

*High Self Esteem (Positive Thinking) Distorts Reality for Temporary Pleasantness ... High Self Regard Involves Openness to the Unpleasant*

## Ego-Weak Mystics and Shamans

In a more recent work, John White (1990) continues Ken Wilber's mistake in not realizing that the sharp distinction between the sacred and the profane that we observe today is a product of recent history.

## The "Holy Fools" of Mystical History Would Not Fare Well in Front of a Psychiatrist

While White refers to early mystics in making his case for what a unitive state of consciousness entails, he does not seem to notice that these people, in terms of his proposition of developing a fully functioning ego as a necessary prerequisite to transpersonal realms, would not only fail in this regard but that by his criteria the kind of odd and extremely eccentric behavior of holy people in the past would be considered insane.

My point is that in neither White's nor Wilber's limited Western viewpoint is there any allowance for that kind of "regressive" behavior on the spiritual path. I quote Feuerstein (1991) as an antidote to this omission:

*It is true that when we look at crazy adepts like Drukpa Kunley or Nityananda, we see phenomenal feats of renunciation. But we also see behavior that, certainly in the eyes of a psychiatrist, at times borders on the neurotic, if not psychotic. Some of these holy fools have in fact wondered about their own sanity. The saintly Ramakrishna, teacher of the world-famous Vivekananda, is a case in point. For a period of time he ceremonially worshipped his own genitals, and on other occasions he installed himself on the altar of the temple where he served as head priest.*

*Such behavior is certainly not "normal." Nor is sitting on garbage heaps or sexually fondling women and girls, as has been reported of several contemporary Hindu adepts. (p. 21)*

# The "Fully Functioning Ego"

Thus, I re-iterate, as White (1990) himself points out (p. xxiv, he says "I elaborate on this central point throughout the book"), central to White's argument that we are evolving into a new species of human at this time in history is that the characteristic Western ego "development" — one could as easily say (and some have said) — "ego-dissociation" — is a necessary prerequisite to higher consciousness. Thus he marshals in, to support his proposal, the concept of the "fully functioning ego" which Wilber has unfortunately popularized.

## A Supremely Defended Ego Is the Aim of Most "Sanitized" Modern Spiritual Pursuits

What these transpersonal theorists are claiming then, in deference to mainstream psychology which is dominated by ego psychologists, is that a fully functioning ego is necessary to develop before one can go on to transpersonal pursuits. My research and experience, confirmed by that of Stanislav Grof and supported by the theory of Michael Washburn (1988) and others, tells me they are wrong in this espousal and that in fact what they are talking about developing is merely a supremely defended ego. It seems that what they would wish to develop is high self-esteem as a prerequisite for higher consciousness.

### But the Idea of Necessary Defenses Is a Relic of Antiquated Freudian Thinking

Yet my research indicates that this is a legacy from Freudian thought which claimed that defenses are necessary. To the contrary, what we have learned from primal therapy and the other experiential, feeling psychotherapies is that defenses *are not* necessary.

## Self Esteem Versus Self Regard

Furthermore, research by Gergen and Marlowe (1969) points out that there is a difference between high self-esteem and high self-regard.

*High Self Esteem (Positive Thinking) Distorts Reality for Temporary Pleasantness ... High Self Regard Involves Openness to the Unpleasant*

Essentially, high self-esteem involves the use of defenses that deny and avoid aspects of reality, whereas high self-regard is based on an openness to and acceptance of those same kinds of unpleasant aspects of reality. Self-esteem and the fully functioning ego is based on distortion of reality and falseness relative to the Self; high self-regard is rooted in painful and not necessarily so functional acceptance of reality in its dark and light, pleasant and unpleasant facets.

*Attunement with the Higher Self Involves a Diminution of the Ego, a Reduction of Ego Defenses*

Similarly, there is a difference between what is often called *ego strength* and what is meant by the fully functioning ego. For ego strength, as Erikson (1968, 1985) uses it for example, is really a consequence of being in tune with the higher self, which is in fact not *ego* strength at all. On the contrary, this kind of attunement with the higher self (or Self) represents a diminution of the ego, a reduction of ego defenses.

## Madness and Genius ... Madness and Mysticism

Going back historically, what is noticeable about mystical adepts (not always their followers, interestingly — see Hesse [1930/1968], for example) is their lack of ego, often from a very early age, and how they are closer to their mystical promptings because of this. This pattern also relates to creative people and the process of creativity. For creative people from all times quite often exhibit this poorly functioning ego that has often been associated with mystics. Because of this, people are familiar with the connection between madness and genius as well as the one between madness and mysticism. (See Erikson, 1962.)

*"Fully Functioning Ego" Actually Precludes, Rather Than Precipitates, the Mystical*

The point is that in neither of these cases is there the development of this recent prescription: "the fully functioning ego." In fact, a fully functioning ego is the last thing a person with mystical promptings would want to develop.

## An Anal-Compulsive Control of Inner Life

One begins to suspect that what these transpersonal theorists and their legions of followers are really saying is that they really do not want to surrender to mystical promptings or to surrender to the Divine.

*Affirmations, Ritual, and the Like Are Capitulation to the Controlling Ego and a Flight from True Spiritual-Mystical Surrender*

What this kind of thinking says about these erstwhile spiritual adepts is that they want to continue to do their controlling; they want to continue to do their affirmations; they want to *control* their inner life. Certainly there are fear reasons why one would want to avoid the path of spiritual surrender and would wish to carry one's controlling and defensive ego over with one into the transpersonal realms. And the devolutional model helps us to see the very deep roots of that fear and makes this entire transpersonal gambit quite understandable.

*Worst of All, These Beliefs Have Roots in Racism and Western Supremacism*

Still, the dictates of truth, and of real spirituality, require that these fearful prescriptions and their illusion-weaving proselytizers be spotlighted for what they are. For it is bad enough when one is self-deluded. It is purely unacceptable when one seeks to foist one's ego defensiveness onto the spiritual pursuits of others. It is worse still when institutions, such as the psychiatric and psychological, are reinforced in their antiquated and soul-destroying methods by such efforts and beliefs. And it is worst of all when these beliefs support the kind of unconscious racism and denigration of other-than-Western-cultures that has caused so much suffering historically.

# 51

# A Mystical Machismo Has Invaded Spiritual Thinking: Whereas Surrender Spiritualities, Believing in Ultimate Goodness, See Controlling as the Problem

*Patriarchal Cultures Carry Their Advance and Conquer Tactics Into the Inner World: Control Versus Surrender*

## Spirituality Is Self-Actualization Not Ego-Actualization

What people like White and Wilber simply do not get is that spirituality is not a matter of further ego-actualization . . . that spirituality involves surrendering the ego, letting go of the ego. Instead they would have us construct, control, strive, to build a "super" ego.

## An Example of This Mistake: Homo Noeticus Is Actually Homo Ego

The *Homo noeticus* that White (1990) describes in his book, *The Meeting of Science of Spirit*, is an example of the kind of mistakes that are possible with this ego-highlighted model of human development. His *Homo noeticus* might better be termed "*Homo ego*." For indeed, what he offers us is a continuation of the Promethean hubris that has brought us to this precarious situation. What he offers us is the same kind of attitude toward the inner world as we have taken towards the outer world, the same kind of advance and conquer, the same kind of control tactics. In support of this I note that while he uses the terms "control" and "master" often — in describing higher states and enlightenment, he uses the terms "surrender" and "letting go" only once. In White's universe I suppose the meek do not inherit the earth.

## Transpersonal Athleticism and Mystical Machismo

This entire attitude is reminiscent of a book from 1968 titled *The Master Game* by Robert S. DeRopp. Theorists like DeRopp, White, and Wilber have never quite understood the idea that this whole spiritual trip is not a matter of transpersonal athleticism, mystical machismo, or jocko-militaristic "mastery." Indeed, it is obvious that White has this attitude in his espousal of the martial arts. It is understandable that he would see spirituality this way in that he is a former military man. Ken Wilber has a strong connection to the military as well, having been brought up in such a family. (Should we really be getting our spiritual advice from the armed forces?)

It is equally clear that White does not quite understand the concept of the surrender of ego for, even in his very espousal of Jesus, he does not accept Jesus's attitude of non-violence or "turn the other cheek." Of course these pacifistic attitudes would not make sense in a spiritual program like his which involves the aggrandizement of the ego and its defense at all costs.

## Spirituality Is Actually Attunement with God, the Giving Up of Ego Struggles

These sorts of would-be spiritual teachers also, in line with the kind of thinking I have described, are the ones who are wont to point out the dangers of regression to "pre-" states and so forth. Once again, in doing so, they acknowledge their fear of loss of ego in their espousal of so-called "higher" or "transcendent" striving. They do not understand that spirituality is, in reality, a matter of attunement with God, attunement with All That Is . . . is a giving up of ego struggles, and a letting go into All That; as opposed to a control, a "mastery," a striving, or a transcendence of it all.

# Control Versus Surrender

Essentially what I am saying is that there are two paths of so-called "spirituality." One of these might be described as going up the "hierarchy of defenses" and the other as undercutting or going below such "act-outs" or spurious "atman projects." Another way of saying this is that there are "control" spiritualities and "surrender" spiritualities, with rarely the twain meeting.

## Control Spiritualities: Atman Projects, Religion, Building a Hierarchy of Defenses — an Egoic Tower of Babel

*Control spiritualities* are adapted to patriarchal cultures and involve the use of the ego to "control" and be in charge of even the realms of the supernatural. This is so because an ultimate evil — a devil or Satan — is postulated, which is given equal weight along with God in determining one's ultimate fate. This type of spirituality is normally what is called *religion.*

## Surrender Spiritualities: God As Being Good; Controlling Is Seen as the Problem, Not the Solution

But there is another brand of spirituality that is based on a belief in the ultimate goodness and rightness of All That Is. God's goodness being essentially the dominant force in the Universe, herein it is considered safe to "surrender" in one's relation to Reality, to expect that one will be guided correctly, in fact perfectly, in the act of letting go. Thus letting go is not to be feared ... as it is in the control spirituality ... but is to be practiced and fostered. In this perspective, which we might call *surrender spirituality*, control is seen as the problem, not the solution.

## "Control" and "Surrender" Psychotherapies

Of course these two approaches to spirituality represent two approaches to psychotherapy as well. The control attitude is the dominant mode of psychoanalytically-based approaches ... in which the "demon" of the *id* is postulated. The attitude of "letting go" and "surrender," on the other hand, is the dominant attitude of the experiential psychotherapies, which are themselves rooted in the tradition of humanistic psychology with its belief in the ultimate goodness of the human organism and which thus allows a faith in the ultimate rightness of human processes.

## Hero's Journey as "Control" Psychotherapy

Since the *control* attitude, in any of its manifestations, requires the postulation of an ultimate evil against which one must remain vigilant and must fight, the common "hero's journey" myth — with its typical fighting and slaying of supposedly evil parts of the personality and reality symbolized as dragons and other monsters — is a prevalent focal myth to this attitude. Corresponding to this myth are the emphasis on disciplines and practices seeking to develop the ego and the will ... over against the dangers that are postulated to exist in the universe requiring these disciplines and, so-called, ego "developments."

## A Different Heroic Response in "Surrender" Paths

Since the "feeling" therapies and the other spiritual and experiential psychotherapeutic modalities with which they are allied are so different in attitude to the traditional "control" attitude, should there not be corresponding differences in myths to exemplify them? Indeed, there are.

In history, the surrender spiritualities have had correspondences in myth in which the dragon is not fought, conquered, and slain, but rather is either tamed and becomes one's ally or one's pet. Saint Margaret is the prime example in the West, but this is a depiction prevalent in the East.

Or else one is swallowed by the "dragon" or monster and, after a while, is reborn. Jonah is the prime example in the West for this latter depiction. But again this reaction to the fearful dissociated aspects of the personality, or the Shadow, is not a common one in the Western patriarchy. However, it is rather prevalent in traditional cultures ... especially in shamanism ... and in the East.

# 52

# The "Patriarchal Mistake" Involves Struggling to Keep Out "Negative" Thoughts: For "There Is No Coming to Consciousness Without Pain" – Carl Jung

*Grof Versus Wilber and the Frantic Thinking Between*
*Paradigms: "Healthy-Mindedness" and the "Sick Soul"*

"There is no coming to consciousness without pain. People will do anything, no matter how absurd, in order to avoid facing their own soul. One does not become enlightened by imagining figures of light, but by making the darkness conscious." – Carl Jung

## "Healthy-Mindedness" and the "Sick Soul"

These two spiritual paths — the controlling and the surrender — were rather distinctively delineated over a hundred years ago by William James (1899/1982) in terms of the spirituality of "healthy mindedness" and that of "the sick soul." The point is that the one — the "healthy mindedness" or control spirituality — involves a kind of *mental* ego-actualization, ego-aggrandizement; and the other — the "sick soul" or surrender spirituality — involves an honest dealing with and processing of the unconscious and all that it is.

## The Patriarchal Mistake in Spirituality ... Keeping Out Negative Thoughts: Whereas True Spirituality Entails Experiencing "Hell" Before Getting to "Heaven"

This second path, this true spirituality involves a going through hell on the way to heaven — which is a matter of surrender and letting go, as opposed to control and healthy-mindedness. The one is a matter of surrendering to All That Is; whereas the delusional path is a matter of defending the ego, continuing ego defenses to keep out negative thoughts, and so on.

It is interesting that the one can always be distinguished from the other in the false one's emphasis on *discipline*, indicating its militaristic attitude of defending against unwanted negative thoughts, and so on. Elsewhere I have called this the "patriarchal mistake" (Adzema, 1972b).

## Stanislav Grof Versus Ken Wilber in Transpersonal Psychology

*John White Genuflects at the Altar of Ken Wilber*

It might be pointed out that these two radically different views of spirituality are exemplified in the transpersonal psychology movement in that surrounding the ideas of Stanislav Grof and that surrounding the ideas of Ken Wilber. It is clear that rarely does the one movement ever refer to or revere the insights of the other. For example, in his book, *The Meeting of Science and Spirit*, John White (1990) does not mention Stanislav Grof at all. Yet he genuflects at the altar of Ken Wilber frequently.

### To Repent Versus to Transcend ... Tob and Metanoia

In this respect, also, we have White's inconsistency in his analysis of the terms *tob* and *metanoia* (and repent). In pointing out that the original Aramaic term for "repent" was *tob* he says that it means "to return" or "to flow back to God." This is fine so far. But then he states that the Greek translation of *tob* is *metanoia* which then means "to transcend." He then forgets the original meaning, disregards it, and builds a theory upon the latter term — meaning that we are to strive, struggle, and travel upward. The entire meaning and significance of returning or flowing back — which would serve to undermine both Wilber's and his theories in its espousal of the significance of the "pre-" state — is completely ignored.

To this move I say, you simply cannot have it both ways: You cannot ascribe some type of greater validity to an earlier term as being closer to the original meaning (*metanoia* over repent), while at the same time ignore or dispute the relevance of the even earlier term, in fact the original one (*tob*), just because to do so would undermine the argument you wish to present!

# Dualistic View of Reality ... Ghost in the Machine Spiritual Thinking

### Inconsistency — Dualism — Matter and Spirit

Nonetheless, perhaps John White's biggest theoretical inconsistency is his assertions of a dual nature to the universe — Matter and Spirit — (with them "interacting"), laid alongside of his assertion that "God is all." He presents therefore a dualistic view of reality much reminiscent of ghost-in-the-machine thinking, with his supposed big advance being that the ghost is just as important as the machine.

## Not a New-Paradigm View

In this respect then, White fails to make the transition to a new-paradigm view. He seems hopelessly caught between the views of competing worlds, trying to assert competing claims, trying to keep his old world from falling apart while still wanting to follow the light he sees ahead. Although he claims to, he does not present a new-paradigm vision.

## Spirit and Matter as Indistinguishable as Ocean and Waves

The point is — as opposed to the old paradigm which says that the world is basically matter and that consciousness is an epiphenomenon of matter — that the new paradigm says the world is basically consciousness or a subjectivity that encompasses All and that the material universe is an epiphenomenon of consciousness. In this world view one does no more need to assert a difference between spirit and matter any more than one can assert a primary distinction between ocean and waves. In this respect we have Sathya Sai Baba's statement that: All there is, is the "I" or the Atma and that this is the foundation for everything else; everything else is illusion. All that really exists is the "I."

This is the same as saying in Western philosophy that subjectivity is the only true reality. This is in line with the philosophical position that the objective reality is indirect perception and is dependent upon subjective reality, and so subjective reality is the only true reality that can be known. (See Adzema, 2013, *Experience Is Divinity: Matter As Metaphor.*)

Unfortunately, White's view is directly contradictory of this — he says that there is danger in "seeing one or the other (matter or spirit) as illusion or delusion" (p. xv). This he does despite the fact that this position of the ultimate phenomenal nature of mundane "common sense" reality is the major conclusion of most of the world's religions, of much of traditional and Platonic philosophy, and more recently, even of the new, quantum, physics.

## The Frantic Theorizing That Goes on in the Time Between Paradigms

In essence then, White's volume presents an example of the kind of frantic hyper-kinetic convoluted theorizing that is known to characterize the transition phase between paradigms. Like the convoluted theories of pre-Copernican astronomers, who struggled fervidly in re-arranging and making room in obsolete theories and concepts for the ever new astronomical data that was pouring in, who were doomed to failure and obsolescence by their inability to grasp the central organizing principle or concept of an Earth that is both round and not the center of the universe; so also White's book, lacking any valid new-paradigm integrating vision, finds itself twisted about itself trying to keep one foot in old-paradigm concepts and theories while stepping with the other into new-paradigm facts and data.

When it comes to paradigm change, you just cannot take both pills.

# 53

# It's Pure Egoism to Think We Are Evolving to a New Consciousness. If We're Lucky We'll Regain the One We've Lost

*Critique of Homo Noeticus: Awareness of Death Leads to Taking Life Spiritually*

## Critique of Homo Noeticus

Finally, I would like to make it clear that all of this is not to say that I do not appreciate White's enthusiasm for advances on the leading edges of science and spirit and for thinking that this might have something to do with an increased pace of changes in consciousness. Indeed, I do believe that we are seeing an incredible and positive change in Western consciousness: But I view these changes, in Wilber's terms, as a translation on the existing "level" as opposed to a "transformation" to a "higher" level, to a "Homo noeticus."

## If We're Lucky We'll Regain the Unity of Consciousness We've Lost

To my way of thinking, there may in fact be pressures to bear upon changing the quality of Western consciousness, and possibly, even probably, in a positive direction. But I believe that these forces have more to do with the effects of our technological advance, in various ways, back upon ourselves.

For example, I believe that modern telecommunications has the effect of making an assault upon ego defenses, making the ego-narrowed, nationalistic or "tribal"-bound views increasingly untenable under an onslaught of information. We might also consider some of the side-effects of pharmaceutical advance. I believe that our exposure to altered states through a variety of prescription and illicit drugs makes narrow, single-state, ego-fortified beliefs and ideas increasingly untenable.

# Awareness of Death Leads to Taking Life Spiritually

I also feel that the negative effects of technological advance — pollution, for example — are having positive effects on Western consciousness, albeit totally inadvertently and fortuitously. In this respect I might note that our co-habitation with the bomb and with environmental destruction is a spur to the growth of consciousness akin to more traditional spiritual paths that speak of the benefits of "having death as an ally."

That is, that the imminent possibility of death is a spur to taking life seriously (and spiritually) and to "waking up" in general.

## Chastened by the Environment We've Created

Another factor is that the declining quality of air and the increased level of toxins that we ingest also are attacks on ego defenses. It is known, for example, that breathing increased amounts of carbon dioxide can bring up primal and perinatal feelings (repressed traumas that our ego defenses normally keep "safely" tucked away in our subconscious). Grof (1993) has described how at one point he explored the use of increased carbon dioxide as a method of inducing nonordinary and perinatal/transpersonal states. The reduction of oxygen apparently acts similarly to a reduction of blood sugar or glucose to the brain and thus results in an inhibition of the brain's ability to keep out unwanted information. The evidence concerning heavy metal toxicity indicates that can have a similar effect (Watson, 1972).

## Down Can Be Up

Now, I do not espouse environmental poisoning as a technique of higher consciousness. But I am saying that apparently Nature ... and we are part of her ... has ways of balancing herself.

And as we edge our way toward global destruction, we increasingly sicken ourselves in the process, causing us to psychologically "go back to the drawing board" and seek solutions — both inner and outer — to our misery. Specifically, I am saying that inhibited brain functioning, whether through oxygen depletion, heavy metal toxicity, or other environmental anomalies has the effect of heightened "mind" functioning (lowered ego and defensive functioning) in the sense of opening us to suppressed individual (and global/universal) truth.

## Acting Out

Granted that many people, especially visible in our big cities, are not integrating this information from outside their ego boundaries (from the unconscious) and sadly are instead acting out the energy of these repressed materials ... which our degenerating environment is opening up to them or giving them access to ... in violent, destructive, wasteful, and pathetic ways.

That is indeed a tragedy and is something that, if that response ends up prevailing, could actually do us in.

## Helping Out

But there are also many people who are integrating this emergent material, regaining their truth and the truths of this planet and the universe, expanding their consciousness to include this information, and carrying that information forward into positive action to heal themselves, the people around them, humanity at large, and the planet.

We can only hope that the forces of integration are more successful than those of disintegration and re-action in the face of this influx of material. That, and then again, that those of us who are dealing positively with these emergent truths can help to build societal structures and processes that make it easier and more likely for those less able to integrate and themselves grow in response to it.

# 54

# Planet of the Apes? Thunderdome? No. But Only If We Are Lucky: Our Primal Return May Indeed Be a Primal Renaissance

*A Grand Synthesis of Natural and Technological*
*Consciousness Is Possible ... But the Ego Fights to the End:*
*Beware of Skinhead Spirituality*

## The Primal Renaissance

So what I am saying is that our advanced technology, itself a product of an unhealthy dissociated ego state that is called Western consciousness, seems, simply fortuitously ... or through the grace of God ... to be having the effect of intense consciousness change — yes! . . . but essentially back in the direction of what has been normal for our species for at least sixty thousand and possibly millions of years but, this time, while retaining ... if we are lucky ... the boons of technology.

## Planet of the Apes? Thunderdome? No. But Only If We Are Lucky

Some people think that the only way our consciousness will return to normal is with the loss of technology and the re-creation of the primal state. Thus they picture "Planet of the Apes" and post-nuclear "Thunderdome" scenarios.

But I believe that we may just be lucky enough ... God may be merciful enough ... to allow us to keep the fruits of the extended Western aberration of consciousness; we may just be allowed to keep some of the toys we acquired from our prodigal days.

There is nothing written in stone, after all, that says that people cannot enjoy the benefits of things produced from "unholy" vessels. Indeed, in the perfect universe that we are beginning to finally re-apprehend, it is clear that all things are useful and to some good end in God's universe.

For example, the legacy and benefits of democracy that we enjoy are not lost or neutralized by our realization that our founding American fathers were chauvinists and slave-owners.

So basically I am saying that I disagree that we are evolving into a new, advanced species, a Homo noeticus. For one thing, it has been pointed out that brain size has actually declined slightly over the past 100,000 years (Winkelman, 1990, p. 28).

## The Primal Return

No. What I believe is that in fact consciousness change is happening ... especially in Western culture ... but in the direction of a return to a more truly human and natural state — one that characterized our species for millions of years.

I am asserting that our Western mental illness, our cultural aberration of consciousness is reversing and healing. However we may be keeping with us, along with our natural self, some fruits of that extended aberration. And these boons we may only fortuitously or through God's grace … and not through any particular heroics or "super" man virtue … be allowed to keep.

Now, that combination of a healthy consciousness and advanced technology may be truly new on this planet. And even of that we cannot be sure. For certainly — and White would agree — likely it has occurred in other places of the universe many times — so that there is no need for species-ego-aggrandizement here, by any means.

## A Grand Synthesis of Which We Should Only Be Grateful

Still, certainly this possibility of a grand synthesis of natural consciousness and scientific-technological acumen is reason for excitement and rejoicing. It is without doubt something we should seek. But there is no need to march in the streets or "we're number 1!" about it. If this is our fortuitous outcome, we have just been lucky. We can only be grateful to the Universe for conspiring to correct our transgressions before we, indeed, "killed us all off"!

# In Light of the Prenatal and Perinatal, Spirituality Re-Visioned

In closing, I wish to say I hope I have conveyed why I believe that the exclusion of the prenatal and perinatal information from Wilber's otherwise comprehensive and laudable schema of transpersonal development leaves it lacking and flawed. I feel that this entire area of integration between the two — the prenatal/perinatal and the transpersonal/spiritual — is considerably more complex and important than has been assumed … certainly that it should not be dismissed, or ignored. Indeed, I feel that the inclusion of pre- and perinatal evidence is crucial for any map of consciousness that purports to be a guide to spiritual evolution.

Cosmic consciousness is not aided by a "fully functioning ego" or by ego-actualization. The age-old admonitions against the lures and enticements, the devices and strategies of ego are as apt in this day as they have always been.

## The Ego Fights to the End

The ego does not surrender easily. It sends out its emissaries of diversion and disruption, of fear and insecurity, to trip up the gullible and the arrogant. Yet surrender is what is required. The tendency to try to control and to ritualize our native experience is what is to be resisted. Banners such as "Homo noeticus" and "fully functioning ego" may bring temporary relief from the difficult task of ego resistance, dismantling of ego defenses, and confrontation with the painful aspects of the unconscious, the Shadow, in the ego-inflation inherent in such standards.

## Beware of Skinhead Spirituality

But it is as wise to align oneself with these tokens to fend off one's necessary insecurity (see Watts, 1951) as it is a good idea to join up with the KKK or the skinheads as a way of dealing with the same kind of insecurities of changing ... and growing ... sociopolitical, cultural, and economic events. In fact the responses are much alike. And they should be equally resisted.

# EPILOGUE

# Are We Entering a Primal Renaissance? The Earliest Yuppies, 25,000 Years Ago, Cast Us Out of the Garden. We Are Returning ... Now

*Out of Eden — Agrarian Revolution ... Return to Eden —*
*Primal Renaissance: Our Greatest Hope May Be the*
*Flourishing of Culture as We Reintegrate Long-Lost*
*Knowledge and Worldview, Formerly Ridiculed as*
*"Primitive"*

We live in exciting times. Information hams it up before us at every turn. This unparalleled info-glut brings fascination, paralysis, agony, insight, change, renewal, and inspiration. In some ways it looks like a renaissance — take the incredible proliferation of technology, for example . . . the mind-boggling advances in computers. But a renaissance of the "primitive," the "uncivilized" . . . a *primal* renaissance? How can that possibly be?

# Paleolithic Consciousness ... Out of Eden

For weeks I had been working on several articles, my ardor suspending me above the landscape of a natural consciousness, a hunter-gatherer one. Called "paleolithic consciousness" by one contemporary theorist, this mindstyle is reputed to exist among our hunter-gatherer progenitors and among some current "primal cultures." It is characterized by greater attunement with body and nature, greater relaxation and well-beingness, more loving child-caring, greater sensory and aesthetic appreciation, more expanded psychic openness, fuller emotional and relational capacity, and greater "with-it-ness" (Witness) with reality in general.

## The Earliest Yuppies and The Agrarian Revolution

I was also focusing on how our civilization came to lose that primal expansiveness of soul — *a la* "ejection from the Garden of Eden." An increasing mistrust of nature — and an inexplicable rebellion against an eternally old "if it ain't broke don't fix it" philosophy — led to attempts to *control* Nature, and consequently body as well. The supposed big "advance" of these earliest yuppies was the domestication of plants and animals. In history, this first major "upwardly mobile" turning is known as the "agrarian revolution," and it occurred variously between ten and thirty-thousand years ago. (See, also, Adzema, 2014, *Planetmates: The Great Reveal.*)

## Renaissance

All of a piece it came to me that what was going on now, in Western culture, was exactly parallel to what had occurred during *the* Renaissance of the fifteenth through seventeenth centuries. At that time, you may recall, the Catholic Church's intellectual hegemony was loosening, which allowed ancient Roman and Greek texts preserved in the monasteries to be released into the collective culture. There, our formerly repressed and forgotten "classical" heritage combined and cross-fertilized with views prevailing at that time to create the incredible flowering of culture and human potential that the word *renaissance* now conveys.

## The View from the Doorstep of Nuclear and Ecological Annihilation

It occurred to me that night how we, in the consciousness and ecology movements, are becoming ever more aware, once again, in diverse and various ways, of the vast legacy of feeling, perception, human fulfillment, and spiritual awareness and viewpoint that current "child-rearing" practices cause us "normally" to leave behind. Similarly we come to realize how much our species lost in coming into its much-vaunted "civilization" in its evolutionary history. The view from the doorstep of nuclear and ecological annihilation allows such perspectives.

Yet, through our different ways of healing ourselves, and to extents greater and lesser, we retrieve that lost and repressed legacy.

## Multiculturalism

And we are, happily, not alone in that retrieval. Increasingly it appears that our age is characterized, on a global scale, by an unprecedented multiculturalism wrought of technological advances in telecommunications and transportation. Consequently, we are pushed to enjoying an ever growing awareness of the legacies of primal cultures, both current and historical.

## Xenophobia Dissolving and "Ego"-Eroding Information

At the same time and not coincidentally we observe our own religious, scientific, and Western-cultural hegemonies collapsing under that same weight of contrary and both xenophobia- and "ego"-eroding information. Moreover, this collapse is aided by momentous and far-reaching occurrences as diverse as our mistaken engagements in third-world countries — our misadventures in Iraq and Vietnam, for example; the technological crisis of credibility wrought of the global ecological crisis; and the discoveries of the new physics with their concurrent death-blow to the pretensions of common-sense materialism.

# Re-Integration of the Primitive and Primal ... Return to Eden

It became clear to me that just as centuries ago we came out from under the thumb of a brand of cultural repression that scapegoated and repressed former cultures — specifically, the Greek and the Roman legacies, calling them "pagan" — we were now coming out from under the thumb of a cultural repression and consequent scapegoating of even longer duration — one extending back ten to thirty-thousand years! Along with this we were seeing not only the limitations and inadequacies of the Western civilization and technology which so many had sacrificed for, and killed for; we were seeing also the re-integration of long-lost knowledge and worldview — which formerly had been obscured and hidden beneath such pejoratives as "primitive," "savage," and "uncivilized."

## Shamans, Vision Quests, Sweat Lodges, and Drums

Some of us were learning this only too well, as it seemed necessary to search out the earliest or least "civilized" cultures possible for the only pertinent tips we could find on sane and healthy child-caring techniques.

But the rest of our culture is catching on too, and in a big way! Shamanistic practices, rites of passage, and indigenous rituals are enjoying great popularity. Workshops on everything from vision quests, fire-walking, and Native American sweat lodges . . . to nature treks, drumming, and "sacred arrow" ceremonies have begun popping up. And currently we are even recognizing our Western patriarchal culture's evil hand in the extermination of society upon society of indigenous peoples; we are re-writing the history books on the legacy of Columbus even as we passed the five-hundredth anniversary of his landing in America.

## A Flourishing of Culture?

What's more, in a manner analogous to the cross-fertilization of ideas that led to the medieval Renaissance, our culture is expanding and becoming richer through the inclusion of these alternate perspectives. Those of us on the healing edge are uniquely able to sense the potential of this inclusion as we experience the effects that this kind of appreciation of the feeling, the affectionate, the intuitive, the natural, the body, and the senses has had upon our individual lives. Why would we not think that this kind of cross-fertilization of repressed heritage would lead to a flourishing of our culture in the same way that it is has led to a blossoming in our lives?

## The Brightest Light on Our Cultural Horizon

Indeed, many of us *do* feel that a "primal renaissance" is occurring on our planet. Furthermore, many of us believe that this occurrence may be, in truth, the brightest hope on what otherwise can appear globally to be a rather bleak social and cultural horizon.

So let us not lose this opportunity to midwife the emergence of this primal renaissance, and, germinal as it may appear at this time, to nurture it to its fullest flowering. We cannot change the past, of course. But our efforts will work — one small measure at least — for righting the many wrongs of those who have come before us toward those earlier primal societies, and the deeply felt ideas and cultural ways they held dear.[1]

# NOTES

## Section One

1. See, for example, my articles, "The Doors of Perception: Each of Us Is Potentially Mind At Large... When Perception Is Cleansed, All Kinds of Nonordinary Things Happen" and "Occupy Science ... A Call for a Scientific Awakening: In Tossing Away Our Species Blinders, We Approach a Truth Far Beyond Science." Both of these articles are available on-line in several places including my blog, *The Great Reveal* and my book, *Experience Is Divinity* (2013).

## Section Two

1. I will be using the terms *primaling* and *feeling one's feelings* interchangeably. We began to use the term *feeling feelings* instead of *primaling* partly to counteract the impression fostered by Janov that all feeling outside of primaling is unreal, that there is a basic difference between primals and normal feelings. Although there is a great difference in quality and intensity, and to that extent a new term is justified, normal feelings are not separate from primal feelings. They are the tip of the iceberg, and are used to get to their roots in primal feelings.

2. The quote is from Spike (1974). See also the interviews in the *Journal of Primal Therapy* (1974) for other changes in the conceptions of early primal.

3. Grof (1980, p. 10) acknowledges the convergence of LSD therapy and primal therapy.

4. Spock is hardly a role model for spirituality ... quite the opposite. Do you not think it awfully convenient that the role models for mysticism promulgated in the media — Unfeeling Machine Men — would be exactly what totalitarian societies want to create?

# Section Five

1. Evidence from experiential psychotherapy is from Graham Farrant's work as reported by him at various APPAH (formerly PPPANA) conferences; in *Aesthema* (1986, 1987); in the International Primal Association Newsletters, winter and summer, 1990; in *Primal Renaissance: The Journal of Primal Psychology* (1995); in works such as Gabriel, 1992; Hannig, 1982; Lake, 1981, 1982; and Noble, 1993; and from personal experience in primal therapy, rebirthing, and holotropic breathwork, among many other sources.

# Section Six

1. There is much variation here, but it would be distracting to go into it too deeply at this point. Suffice it to say that everyone's experience in the womb is not so marvelous. Too frequently — and more frequently in modern times with the advent of wide-scale drug use, unwanted pregnancies, and unnatural and chemicalized food supplies — the secondary shutdown-dualism occurs much earlier in pregnancy. The encounter with a "world-obstacle" and a "frustration" of fetal intention can occur even in very early stages of fetal development. In such cases, later womb experience takes

on hellish tones and this has far-reaching ramifications throughout all later life ... not to mention, for society.

2. This statement is in direct contradiction to Wilber's later formulations of his theory (1980 and on) because he claims that matter, existing as body, is a lowest form of consciousness. I point this out because this discrepancy demonstrates clearly how he has unconsciously accepted the primacy-of-the-physical-universe postulate of the Newtonian-Cartesian paradigm. The resulting epiphenomenalism is evident in his statements that "the great chain of being . . . can be listed as matter to body to soul to spirit" and that "you are born with a material body, but eventually a fully developed mind emerges . . . [later] when the soul emerges . . . [later] when the spirit emerges" (1989, p. 463).

Thus, it seems that, despite the impressively presented new-paradigm vision he brings to us in *The Spectrum of Consciousness*, Wilber's later formulations crumple under the weight of old-paradigm developmental theorists (see Wilber, 1980) whose theories are based on the idea that mind evolves out of matter, that consciousness is an epiphenomenon of brain activity and not the reverse.

Swayed in this way by the kind of thinking that seeks to understand body (and mind) from the outside — as separate object — the new-paradigm understanding that matter and body are metaphorical reflections of Consciousness fades in its influence on his formulations. Furthermore, swayed by developmentalists that, in typical Western linear style, *assume* a progression through time; the new-paradigm viewing point of the Eternal Moment, of the illusory nature of time and, consequently, of the controversial character of cause and effect is also lost in Wilber's writings.

3. It must be admitted that these biological underpinnings, as universal as they would seem to be, are to some degree culturally affected. These biocultural influences arise through what the mother eats, drinks or doesn't drink, smokes or doesn't, uses or doesn't, thinks, and feels during the course of the pregnancy. For

these biocultural influences on consciousness see Verny (1981; 1987), Noble (1993), Janov's later writings (e.g., 1973, 1975, 1983), the *Journal of Primal Therapy*, and publications of the Association for Pre- and Perinatal Psychology and Health (APPPAH), especially the *Pre- and Perinatal Psychology Journal*.

4. I realize that Wilber later changed from his position in *The Spectrum of Consciousness* concerning the Centaur. In later works he has claimed that the Centaur should be reserved for only the adult post-ego period. This change highlights our philosophical differences. Obviously my analysis here, based upon pre- and perinatal psychology, supports his earlier position and strongly disputes his later one. It underscores what I consider a glaring discrepancy on his part. For he both acknowledges a pre-birth existence for soul and consciousness (1980, pp. 160-176) but then constructs his structures of development in a typical Western anti-reincarnational and anti- new-paradigm way as if *that pre-birth existence does not exist* (and both in the same work).

This contradiction may be partly due to his source of prenatal psychology being the *Tibetan Book of the Dead*. I get the sense that his use of such a "spiritual" source — as opposed to our empirical Western experiential ones — has somehow prevented him from taking seriously the notion that the person "really" does exist prior to the time of birth. For instance, he puts quotes around *events* when discussing the happenings before birth (1980, p. 162), indicating the dubious category he has assigned them. Also, he says that one may consider these events metaphorically, symbolically, or mythically (1980, p. 162). Obviously, prenatal — as well as past-life — psychology affirms the importance of taking such a notion and such prenatal events seriously and regrets his later formulations.

# Section Seven

1. In regard to a connection between our personal experience and the way we see the physical world — as in this example, conjuring the idea of a "Big Bang" origin — see *Experience Is Divinity*

(2013), Part 2, "Matter As Metaphor," especially Chapter 22, "The World Is Rife with Messages — Personal and Universal — Regarding the Meaning of Existence, Our Place in the Universe, and Guidance for Getting Us hOMe." Also see Roger Jones's (1982) *Physics As Metaphor*.

# Section Nine

1. Related information about the Mbuti is brought out in an on-line article by James R. Coffey. They include some tantalizing details of particular importance in light of prenatal and perinatal psychology and the falls from grace. In "The Mbuti of Central Africa: The Only Known Egalitarian Society (with Rare Video)," Coffey writes,

*...the Mbuti have no rulers, no political structure, and except for a religion that essentially ties them functionally and ritually to the forest, they have no cohesive social structure. Most significantly, every man, woman, and child has equal access to resources — which is the very definition of egalitarian.*

*Men and women have equal power, decisions are made by group consensus, and minor disputes are usually dealt with by ridicule, gossip, or shunning....*

*...the fact that their social structure promotes gendered equality does not prevent individuals from attempting to promote hierarchy; they are simply ignored and considered insane.*

*...one point of particular distinction in Mbuti society is that children have what could be considered an irrational amount of power in ritual situations — believed to be most closely connected to the primal spirits of the forest.*

*...most Mbuti villages (which are usually comprised of only a few essential huts), are laid out to represent a human female womb in shape and design. This is so that when entering and exiting the village (and*

*each hut), you are symbolically reborn — of your mother and of the forest.*

*...the village and physical use of space is thought of as male (in concept), while the exact layout, shape of the huts, and actual utilization of the space is thought of as female. Thus, it is a constant representation of sexual interaction, reflecting both human physical intercourse as well as symbolic birth by way of the forest....* (full article available on-line)

Also see, on the internet on the site *Peaceful Societies: Alternatives to Violence and War*, the post titled "Encyclopedia of Selected Peaceful Societies: Mbuti." Quoting from the article,

*Beliefs that Foster Peacefulness. The Mbuti view their forest as a sacred, peaceful place to live — they constantly refer to it with not only reverence but adoration. They sing songs to it, in appreciation for the care and goodness they feel they get from it. If something goes wrong in their camp at night, such as an invasion of army ants, the problem is that the forest is sleeping, so they sing to awaken it. Their songs of rejoicing, devotion, and praise serve to make the forest happy. They do not believe in evil spirits or sorcery from the forest as the nearby villagers do — their forest world is kinder than that.*

*Avoiding and Resolving Conflict. Normally the Mbuti settle conflicts with quick actions. One of their major strategies is laughter, jokes, and ridicule. The camp clown, an individual who assumes the responsibility of trying to end conflicts through ridicule, uses mime and antics to re-focus the conflict on himself, to get everyone laughing and ridiculing, in order to divert attention from the issue of the moment. The Mbuti have no formal methods for resolving disputes or crimes, and no individual would pass a sentence on another. But if one person is clearly in the wrong, an entire camp can react by punishing, perhaps even thrashing, an offender. Sometimes parties to a dispute might settle it through arguments or mild fighting. Ostracism is always a possibility, but it is rare.*

*Gender Relations.* Mbuti men who still live in the Ituri Forest organize and control the net hunting, though the women help them. The women gather vegetable foods in the forests, such as mushrooms ... but the men will help out. The women freely join discussions with men, though tensions between the sexes do arise. One strategy they use to diffuse gender tensions is to have a "tug of war," the men and boys opposite the women and girls. If the males begin to win, a man will leave his side and join the women, mockingly encouraging them in a falsetto voice. When that group begins to win, a woman drops off her side and joins the men, encouraging them in a deep bass voice to greater efforts. The fun and ridicule grow as the contest continues, until everyone dissolves into hysterical laughter. The effect is to ridicule aggression, competitiveness, and conflict itself. Both sexes will do whatever they can to survive and support their families in the refugee camps.

*Raising Children.* A Mbuti mother develops a special lullaby that she starts singing to her baby while the infant is still in the womb. She reassures the child about the world into which he or she will soon be born, with descriptions of the goodness of the forest and the supportiveness of the human environment. As they grow older, children learn to play non-competitive games that emphasize cooperative activities. Sometimes children are spanked and slapped by their parents....

*Strategies for Avoiding Warfare and Violence.* Different groups of Pygmies try to avoid warfare with one another. One incident that occurred during the honey-gathering season indicates this tendency. With everyone spread out through the forest in small groups to gather the honey, the Mbuti suddenly realized that a foreign Pygmy group had invaded their territory and were stealing honey from their trees. One man became excited and tried to summon everyone to make war on the invaders. But another man explained that they invade each other's territories every year, and no harm is done as long as the different groups don't encounter one another. If they do have a chance encounter, the invaders simply flee back to their own territory, leaving *behind everything they have stolen.* (full article available on-line)

In other places the Mbuti have been put forth as a possible model for exemplary parenting and care of children.

Also see, on the site, *Peaceful Societies: Alternatives to Violence and War*, the post of May 9, 2013 titled "Mbuti Cherish the Forest — Does Anyone Care?" It refers to a heart-breaking video, available on-line, along with the article. Quoting,

*This 5:44 minute video, just released to Vimeo last week, was clearly prepared as a way of celebrating with viewers the traditional skills and lives of the Mbuti, and, just as importantly, of raising awareness about the stresses and traumas those people are enduring....*

*"Everyone is important in the hunt," he tells us, with a fetching image of a Mbuti woman and a baby on her back on the screen. He describes how the hunters stretch their nets through the forest, and how the women and children make enough noise to drive animals into the nets for the men to kill. Then, he says, "we divide the meat into small pieces so that everyone in the group can have some." Their forest tradition clearly includes fond memories of the custom of sharing.*

*Another man, identified as Chief Mangubo, takes over and tells us about the importance of the ancestors, and of music, to the Mbuti. The people play, dance, and sing every day as a way of communicating with their ancestors, he says. They welcome a new baby into the community through the performance of a special dance. They sing to insure the success of the honey collection season, they sing to celebrate marriages, to accompany their initiation rituals, and sometimes just to show their happiness. If problems come up, they hope their songs will elicit assistance from the ancestors....*

*...the closing credits indicate that armed guerillas attacked the Okapi Wildlife Reserve headquarters in June 2012 in retaliation for the efforts of the park guards to cut down on the poaching, which is decimating the*

*wildlife. The fighters raped dozens of women, killed six people, and took over 50 hostages. They looted and burned the buildings. People that could, fled into the forest. The Mbuti featured in the video, people who lived near the park headquarters, have disappeared, and their whereabouts are still unknown.* (full article available on-line, along with the video, *Mbuti: Children of the Forest,* from JH Wildlife Film Festival on Vimeo.)

# Section Ten

1. The new prenatal and perinatal information is referenced many times in this book — see especially Section One — as well as in publications and conferences of the Association for Pre- and Perinatal Psychology and Health (APPPAH); the writings of Thomas Verny (1981, 1987); the evidence from primal therapy, rebirthing, holotropic breathwork, and psychedelic research — published in places too numerous to mention; and so on.

# Epilogue

1. For more along these lines, look to the next book in this Return to Grace series. *Prodigal Human: The Descent of Man,* Return to Grace, Volume 10, is scheduled for publication in 2015. Portions of it are already available on-line, however; and more will be added over time, between now and publication time. Doing an internet search for *Prodigal Human* along with my name should yield fruitful results.

# REFERENCES

Adzema, M. (1970). *The dangers of mysticism for modern youth.* P.O. Box 40372, Eugene, OR 97404. Unpublished manuscript.

Adzema, M. (1972a). The way forward is down. P.O. Box 40372, Eugene, OR 97404. Unpublished paper.

Adzema, M. (1972b). *The centered path through hell.* P.O. Box 40372, Eugene, OR 97404. Unpublished manuscript.

Adzema, Michael. (1981). *Womb with a view: Spiritual aspects of intrauterine experience.* P.O. Box 40372, Eugene, OR 97404. Unpublished manuscript.

Adzema, Michael. (1984). *Cells with a view: Spiritual and philosophical aspects of sperm and egg experience.* P.O. Box 40372, Eugene, OR 97404. Unpublished manuscript.

Adzema, M. (1985). A primal perspective on spirituality. *Journal of Humanistic Psychology, 25*(3), 83-116.

Adzema, M. (1993). *Primal renaissance: The emerging millennial return.* Rohnert Park, CA: Sillygod Press.

Adzema, M. (1994). *Falls from grace: Child 'development' in transpersonal context and a devolutional model of consciousness.* Published Master's Thesis, Sonoma State University, Rohnert Park, CA.

Adzema, M. (1995). Biologically constituted realities: An anti-anthropocentric (species-relative) and new paradigm perspective. *Primal Renaissance: The Journal of Primal Psychology, 1*(1).

Adzema, M. (2013). *Experience is divinity: Matter as metaphor.* Eugene, OR: CreateSpace.

Adzema, M. (2014). *Planetmates: The great reveal.* Eugene, OR: CreateSpace.

Adzema, M. (2015, forthcoming; partly available on-line now). *Prodigal Human.* P.O. Box 40372, Eugene, OR 97404.

Amodeo, J. (1981). Focusing applied to a case of disorientation in meditation. *Journal of Transpersonal Psychology, 13*(2), 149-154.

Baba, S. S. (1991). *Sanatha Sarathi*, November, 295.

Bache, C. (1981). On the emergence of perinatal symptoms in Buddhist meditation. *Journal for the Scientific Study of Religion, 20*(4), 339-350.

Baker, J. P. (1986). *Conscious conception: Elementary journey through the labyrinth of sexuality.* Monroe, UT: Freestone.

Benoit, H. (1955). *The supreme doctrine.* New York: The Viking Press.

Berman, M. (1986). Cybernetic dream. *Journal of Humanistic Psychology, 26*(2), 24-51.

Bird-David, N. (1992). Beyond "the original affluent society": A culturalist reformulation. *Current Anthropology, 33*(1), 25-47.

Buchheimer, A. (1983, July). Memory-preverbal and verbal. Paper presented at the meeting of the 1st International Congress of Pre- and Perinatal Psychology, Toronto, Ontario.

Buchheimer, A. (1987). Graham Farrant interviewed at Appel Farm, Sunday, August 31, 1986. *Aesthema: The Journal of the International Primal Association*, No.7, 40-45.

Carter, B. (1993). Separation, reunification in cell division, conception, birth, myth, rite and consciousness. Presentation at The Creativity of the Human Psyche: Third Annual Conference of the Association for Holotropic Breathwork International, May 2, 1993, in San Rafael, California.

Castaneda, C. (1977). *The second ring of power*. New York: Simon & Schuster.

Chamberlain, D. (1988). *Babies remember birth*. New York: Ballantine.

Cheek, D. B. and LeCron, L. M. (1968). *Clinical hypnotherapy*. New York: Grune & Stratton.

deMause, L. (1982). *The foundations of psychohistory*. New York: Creative Roots.

deMause, L. (1987). The fetal origins of history. In Verny, T. (ed.) *Pre- and Perinatal Psychology*, New York: Human Sciences Press, 243-259.

De Ropp, R. S. (1968). *The master game*. New York: Delecorte Press.

Earle, J. (1981). Cerebral laterality and meditation: A review of the literature. *Journal of Transpersonal Psychology, 13*(2), 155-173.

Eddington, A. S. (1928). *The nature of the physical world*. London: Allen and Unwin Ltd. and The Macmillan Company.

Epstein, M., & Leiff, J. (1981). Psychiatric complications of meditation practice. *Journal of Transpersonal Psychology, 13*(2), 137-147.

Erikson, E. H. (1962). *Young man Luther*. New York: W. W. Norton & Co.

Erikson, E. H. (1968). *Identity: Youth and crisis*. New York: W. W. Norton & Co.

Erikson, E. H. (1985). *Childhood and society*. New York: W. W. Norton & Co.

Farrant, G. (1987). Cellular consciousness. *Aesthema: The Journal of the International Primal Association, No.7* [January, 1987], 28-39.

Feher, L. (1980). *The psychology of birth*. London: Souvenir Press.

Feuerstein, G. (1991). For God's sake: Reflections on religious extremism. *The Quest, 4*(3), 17-22.

Fodor, N. (1949). *Search for the beloved*. New Hyde Park, NJ: University Books.

Fodor, N. (1951). *New approach to dream interpretation*. New Hyde Park, NJ: University Books.

French, M. (1985). *Beyond power: On women, men, and morals*. New York: Ballantine Books.

Freud, S. (1959). *Inhibitions, symptoms and anxiety*. New York: W. W. Norton. (Originally published, 1927).

Fromm, E. (1955). *The sane society*. New York: Rinehart.

Fromm, E., Suzuki, D. T., & DeMartino, R. (1970). *Zen Buddhism and psychoanalysis*. New York: Harper & Row.

Gabriel, M. (1992). *Voices from the womb*. Lower Lake, CA: Aslan Publishing Co.

Gardiner, Patrick. (1967). Arthur Schopenhauer (1788-1860). In *Encyclopedia of Philosophy*.

Gergen, K.J., & Marlowe, D. (1969). Personality and social interaction. In *Handbook of social psychology, Vol III* (G. Lindzey & E. Aronson, Eds.). Reading, MA: Addison-Wesley, pp. 590-665.

Gregor, T. (1985). *Anxious pleasures: The sexual lives of the Amazonian People*. Chicago: University of Chicago Press.

Grof, S. (1970). Beyond psychoanalysis I: Implications of LSD research for understanding dimensions of human personality. *Darshana International, 10*(3), 55-73.

Grof, S. (1976). *Realms of the human unconscious*. New York: Dutton.

Grof, S. (1980). *LSD psychotherapy*. Pomona, CA: Hunter House.

Grof, S. (1985). *Beyond the brain: Birth, death and transcendence in psychotherapy*. Albany, NY: State University of New York Press.

Grof, S. (1988). *The adventure of self-discovery: Dimensions of consciousness and new perspectives in psychotherapy and inner exploration*. Albany, NY: State University of New York Press.

Grof, S. (1993). From presentation on holotropic breathwork in Grof Transpersonal Training module, July, 1993.

Grof, S., and Grof, C. (1989). (eds.) *Spiritual emergency: When personal transformation becomes a crisis*. Los Angeles: Jeremy P. Tarcher.

Grof, S., and Grof, C. (1990). *The stormy search for the self: A guide to personal growth through transformational crisis.* Los Angeles: Jeremy P. Tarcher.

Grof, S., and Halifax, J. (1977). *The human encounter with death.* New York: Dutton.

Hannig, P. (1982). *Feeling people: A revolutionary concept in therapy, lifestyle and human contact.* Winter Park, FL: Anna Publishing Inc.

Heider, J. (1974). Catharsis in human potential encounter. *Journal of Humanistic Psychology, 14*(4), 27-47.

Hesse, H. (1951). *Siddhartha.* Trans. by Hilda Rosner. New York: New Directions.

Hesse, H. (1968). *Narcissus and Goldmund.* Trans. by Ursule Molinaro. New York: Farrar, Straus and Giroux. (Originally published, 1930).

Huxley, A. (1954). *The doors of perception and heaven and hell.* New York: Harper & Row.

I Ching or Book of Changes (1950). (R. Wilhelm & C. F. Baynes, Trans.).

Irving, M. C. (1988). *Natalism and the serpent/dragon image and myth: A study in art, mythology, and pre- and perinatal psychology.* 274 Rhodes Avenue, Toronto, Ontario, Canada, M4L 3A3. Unpublished manuscript.

James, W. (1982). *The varieties of religious experience.* New York: Viking Penguin. (Originally published, 1899).

Janov, A. (1970). *The primal scream: Primal therapy, the cure for neurosis.* New York: Dell.

Janov, A. (1971). *The anatomy of mental illness*. New York: Berkeley.

Janov, A. (1972). *The primal revolution*. New York: Simon & Schuster.

Janov, A. (1973). The nature of consciousness. *Journal of Primal Therapy, 1*(1), 7-63.

Janov, A. (1973). *The feeling child*. New York: Simon & Schuster.

Janov, A. (1974a). Further implications of "levels of consciousness." *Journal of Primal Therapy, 1*(4), 313-352.

Janov, A. (1974b) The nature of pain and its relation to levels of consciousness. *Journal of Primal Therapy, 2*(1), 5-50.

Janov, A. (1980). *Prisoners of pain*. Garden City, NY: Doubleday.

Janov, A. (1983). *Imprints: The lifelong effects of the birth experience*. New York: Coward-McCann.

Janov, A. and Holden, E. M. (1975). *Primal man: The new consciousness*. New York: Crowell.

Johnson, B. (1991). A primal religion. *Aesthema: The Journal of the International Primal Association, No. 10* [February 1991], 51-58.

Jones, R. S. (1982). *Physics as metaphor*. Minneapolis, MN: The University of Minnesota.

*Journal of Primal Therapy* (1974). Primal people. *2*(1&2), 79-88, 156-173.

Kapleau, P. (1980). *The three pillars of Zen*. Garden City, NY: Doubleday.

Kasturi, N. (1991). *Sanatha Sarathi*, November, 295.

Kaufmann, W. (1974). An anatomy of the primal revolution. *Journal of Humanistic Psychology, 14*(4), 49-62.

Keen, S. (1972). Field report: Janov and primal therapy. *Psychology Today*, February 1972, 43-46, 86, 88, 89.

Kelley, C. (1972). Post-primal and genital character: A critique of Janov and Reich. *Journal of Humanistic Psychology, 12*(2), 61-73.

Keniston, K. (1968). *Young radicals: Notes on committed youth.* New York: Harcourt, Brace & World.

Kornfield, J. (1979). Intensive insight meditation: A phenomenological study. *Journal of Transpersonal Psychology, 11*(1), 41-58.

Labbe, A. 1991. Consciousness versus awareness in the light of classical Eastern perspectives on the nature of transcendence. Paper delivered at the 1991 Annual Conference of the Society for the Anthropology of Consciousness, March 21, 1991.

Lake, F. (1981). *Tight corners in pastoral counseling.* London: Darton, Longman and Todd.

Lake, F. (1982). *The first trimester.* Unpublished manuscript.

Lake, F. (1986). *Clinical theology: A theological and psychological basis to clinical pastoral care.* London: Darton, Longman, and Todd. (Originally published, 1966).

Larimore, T. (1990a). Six body movements expressed in cellular consciousness and their meanings — part I. *IPA Newsletter: International Primal Association*, winter, 1990, 9.

Larimore, T. (1990b). Six body movements expressed in cellular consciousness and their meanings — part II. *IPA Newsletter: International Primal Association*, summer, 1990, 8.

Larimore, T., and Farrant, G. (1995). "Egg and Sperm Memory: Universal Body Movements in Cellular Consciousness and What They Mean" *Primal Renaissance: The Journal of Primal Psychology, 1*(1) [Spring, 1995].

Lawlor, R. (1991). *Voices of the first day: Awakening in the aboriginal dreamtime*. Rochester, VT: Inner Traditions International.

Leboyer, F. (1975). *Birth without violence*. London: Wildwood House.

Liedloff, J. (1977). *The continuum concept: Allowing human nature to work successfully*. Reading, MA: Addison-Wesley.

Lonsbury, J. (1978). Inside primal therapy. *Journal of Humanistic Psychology, 18*(4), 19-28.

Lyn-Piluso, Geraldine, and Lyn-Piluso, Gaetano. (1994). Organic parenting. *Aesthema: The Journal of the International Primal Association, No. 11* [July 1994]

Mahler, M. S.; Pine, F.; and Bergman, A. (1975). *The psychological birth of the human infant*. New York: Basic Books.

Maslow, A. H. (1968). *Toward a psychology of being*. New York: Van Nostrand Reinhold Company.

Masters, R., & Houston, J. (1967). *The varieties of psychedelic experience*. New York: Dell.

McCloud, J. (1975). *Beyond anger, beyond sadness*. Unpublished manuscript.

Mott, F. (1960). *The nature of the self: The human mind rediscovered as a specific instance of a universal configuration governing all integration*. London: Allan Wingate.

Mott, F. (1964). *The universal design of creation*. Edenbridge, England: Mark Beech.

Muktananda, B. (1974). *The play of consciousness*. Oakland, CA: SYDA Foundation.

Muller, W. (1992). *Legacy of the heart: The spiritual advantages of a painful childhood*. New York: Simon and Schuster.

Noble, E. (1993). *Primal connections: How our experiences from conception to birth influence our emotions, behavior, and health*. New York: Simon and Schuster.

Pearce, J. C. (1980). *Magical child: Rediscovering nature's plan for our children*. Toronto: Bantam.

Peerbolte, M. L. (1954). *Prenatal dynamics*. Leyden, Netherlands: Uitgeverij Sijthoff.

Raheem, A. (1991). *Soul return: Integrating body, psyche & spirit*. Boulder Creek, CA: Aslan Publishing.

Rajneesh, B. S. (1976). *Meditation: The art of ecstasy*. New York: Harper & Row.

Rama, S.; Ballentine, R.; and Ajaya, S. (1976). *Yoga and psychotherapy*. Glenview, Il: Himalayan Institute.

Rank, O. (1952). *The trauma of birth*. New York: Robert Brunner. (Originally published, 1929).

Robinson, J. M. (Ed.). (1988). *The Nag Hammadi Library in English, revised edition*. San Francisco: Harper & Row.

Rowan, J. (1983). The real self and mystical experiences. *Journal of Humanistic Psychology, 23*(2), 9-27.

Rowan, John. (1992). Hegel and self-actualization. *The Humanistic Psychologist, 20*(1), 58-74.

Sahlins, Marshall. (1972). *Stone age economics.* London: Tavistock.

St. John of the Cross. (1959). *The dark night of the soul.* (E. A. Peters, Trans.). Garden City, NY: Doubleday.

Schneider, Kirk. (1987). The deified self: A "centaur" response to Wilber and the transpersonal movement. *Journal of Humanistic Psychology, 27*(2), 196-216.

Sheldrake, R. (1981). *A new science of life: The hypothesis of formative causation.* Los Angeles: Jeremy P. Tarcher.

Sheldrake, R. (1991a). Is nature alive? *Human Potential*, 16-21, 33-39.

Sheldrake, R. (1991b). The rebirth of nature: The greening of science and God. New York: Bantam.

Shoham, S. G. (1979). *Salvation through the gutters.* New York: Hemisphere Publications.

Shoham, S. G. (1979). *The myth of Tantalus.* St. Lucia: The University of Queensland Press.

Shoham, S. G. (1990). The bridge to nothingness: Gnosis, Kabbala, Existentialism, and the Transcendental Predicament of Man. *ReVision, 13*(1) [Summer 1990], 33-45.

Spike. (1974). After the scream. *Journal of Primal Therapy, 1*(3), 269-272.

Sroufe, L. A.; Cooper, R. G.; and DeHart, G. B. (1992). *Child development: Its nature and course*. New York: McGraw-Hill.

Stettbacher, J. K. (1991). *Making sense of suffering: The healing confrontation with your own past*. New York: Dutton.

Turnbull, C. M. (1961). *The forest people: A study of the Pygmies of the Congo*. New York: Simon & Schuster.

Turnbull, C. M. (1972). *The mountain people*. New York: Simon and Schuster.

Van der Post, L. (1986). *The lost world of the Kalahari*. New York: Harcourt Brace Jovanovich.

Verny, T. (1984). Birth and sexuality. *Aesthema, 4,* 48-55.

Verny, T., (Ed.). (1987). *Pre- and perinatal psychology*. New York: Human Sciences Press.

Verny, T., and Kelly, J. (1981). *The secret life of the unborn child*. New York: Dell.

Walsh, R. (1979). Meditation research: An introduction and review. *Journal of Transpersonal Psychology, 11*(2), 161-174.

Wambach, H. (1979). *Life before life*. New York: Bantam Books.

Wasdell, D. (1979). *Towards a unified field theory of human behavior*. London: URCHIN (Unit for Research into Changing Institutions) Meridian House, 115 Poplar High Street, London E14 OAE.

Wasdell, D. (1985a). *Primal perspective*. London: URCHIN (Unit for Research into Changing Institutions) Meridian House, 115 Poplar High Street, London E14 OAE.

Wasdell, D. (1985b). *Foundations of psycho-social analysis*. London: URCHIN (Unit for Research into Changing Institutions) Meridian House, 115 Poplar High Street, London E14 OAE.

Wasdell, D. (1990). *The roots of social insanity: The pre- and perinatal ground of socio-political dynamic*. London: URCHIN (Unit for Research into Changing Institutions) Meridian House, 115 Poplar High Street, London E14 OAE.

Washburn, M. (1988). *The ego and the dynamic ground: A transpersonal theory of human development*. Albany, NY: SUNY Press.

Washburn, M. (1990). Two patterns of transcendence. *Journal of Humanistic Psychology, 30*(3), 84-112.

Watson, G. (1972). *Nutrition and your mind: The psychochemical response*. New York: Harper & Row.

Watts, A. W. (1951). *The wisdom of insecurity*. New York: Vintage Books.

White, J. (1990). *The meeting of science and spirit*. New York: Paragon House.

Whiting, J., and Child, I. (1953). *Child training and personality: A cross-cultural study*. New Haven, Ct: Yale University Press.

Wilber, K. (1977). *The spectrum of consciousness*. Wheaton, IL: Theosophical Publishing House.

Wilber, K. (1980). *The atman project*. Wheaton, IL: Theosophical Publishing House.

Wilber, K. (1982). The pre/trans fallacy. *Journal of Humanistic Psychology, 22*(2), 5-43.

Wilber, K. (1983). *A sociable God*. Boulder, CO: Shambhala Publishing.

Wilber, K. (1989). God is so damn boring: A response to Kirk Schneider. *Journal of Humanistic Psychology, 29*(4), 457-469.

Winkelman, M. (1990). The evolution of consciousness: An essay review of *Up from Eden* (Wilber 1981). *Anthropology of Consciousness, 1*(3-4):24-31.

Winnicott, D. W. (1958). *Collected papers: Through paediatrics to psycho-analysis*. New York: Basic Books.

Yogananda, P. (1946). *Autobiography of a yogi*. Los Angeles: Self-Realization Fellowship.

# ABOUT THE AUTHOR

Michael Adzema is a writer, activist, teacher, and psychotherapist, specializing in primal therapy, breathwork, and rebirthing. He was the editor of *Primal Renaissance* — a professional journal of primal psychology — and was the first person in the United States to teach prenatal and perinatal psychology at the university level, which he did at Sonoma State University in the early Nineties. In the early Eighties, working as an anti-nuke activist with Oregon Fair Share, he was one of a small group of people whose actions led to the lawsuit that ended nuclear plant construction in the United States.

Over the last fifteen years, Michael Adzema has managed and authored a number of popular websites and blogs, including *Primal Spirit; Becoming Authentic; The Great Reveal by the Planetmates; Apocalypse NO; Culture War, Class War;* and *Things That Want to Be Said.*

In addition to *Falls from Grace,* he has authored the books, *Experience Is Divinity; Planetmates, The Great Reveal; Apocalypse NO; Primal Renaissance; Culture War, Class War;* and the companion volume to *Apocalypse NO,* titled *Apocalypse Emergency — Love's Wake-Up Call.*

Along with all the books mentioned above, except *Primal Renaissance,* four more books are to be published in his Return to Grace series, for a total of ten volumes, being released in 2013 through 2015.